RAND MCNALLY

QUICK REFERENCE

WORLD ATLAS

Quick Reference World Atlas
Copyright © 1995 by Rand McNally & Company.
Revised 1996 Printing.

Printed in the United States of America.

Library of Congress Catalog Number: 95-067031

World Political Information Table

This table gives the area, population, population density, political status, capital, and predominant languages for every country in the world. The political units listed are categorized by political status in the form of government column of the table, as follows: A—independent countries; B—internally independent political entities which are under the protection of another country in matters of defense and foreign affairs; C—colonies and other dependent political units; and D—the major administrative subdivisions of Australia, Canada, China, the United Kingdom, and the United States. For comparison, the table also includes the continents and the world. All footnotes appear at the end of the table.

The populations are estimates for January 1, 1994, made by Rand McNally on the basis of official data, United Nations estimates, and other available information. Area figures include inland water.

Region or Political Division	Area Sq. Mi.	Est. Pop. 1/1/94	Pop. Per. Sq. Mi.	Form of Government and Ruling Power	Capital	Predominant Languages
Afars and Issas see Djibouti						
† Afghanistan	251,826	16,595,000	66	Islamic republic A	Kābul	Dari, Pashto, Uzbek, Turkmen
Africa	11,700,000	683,700,000	58			
Alabama	52,423	4,202,000	80	State (U.S.) D	Montgomery	English
Alaska	656,424	597,000	0.9	State (U.S.) D	Juneau	English, indigenous
† Albania	11,100	3,424,000	308	Republic A	Tiranë	Albanian, Greek
Alberta	255,287	2,599,000	10	Province (Canada) D	Edmonton	English
† Algeria	919,595	26,780,000	29	Provisional military government A	Algiers (El Djazaïr)	Arabic, Berber dialects, French
American Samoa	77	53,000	688	Unincorporated territory (U.S.) C	Pago Pago	Samoan, English
† Andorra	175	58,000	331	Parliamentary co-principality (Spanish and French B	Andorra	Catalan, Spanish (Castilian), French
† Angola	481,354	11,040,000	23	Republic A	Luanda	Portuguese, indigenous
Anguilla	35	7,000	200	Dependent territory (U.K. protection) B	The Valley	English
Anhui	53,668	58,850,000	1,097	Province (China) D	Hefei	Chinese (Mandarin)
Antarctica	5,400,000	(1)				
† Antigua and Barbuda	171	64,000	374	Parliamentary state A	St. John's	English, local dialects
† Argentina	1,073,519	33,635,000	31	Republic A	Buenos Aires and Viedma (4)	Spanish, English, Italian, German, French
Arizona	114,006	3,943,000	35	State (U.S.) D	Phoenix	English
Arkansas	53,182	2,438,000	46	State (U.S.) D	Little Rock	English
† Armenia	11,506	3,743,000	325	Republic A	Yerevan	Armenian, Russian
Aruba	75	68,000	907	Self-governing territory (Netherlands protection) B	Oranjestad	Dutch, Papiamento, English, Spanish
Ascension	34	1,000	29	Dependency (St. Helena) C	Georgetown	English
Asia	17,300,000	3,385,900,000	196			
† Australia	2,966,155	17,950,000	6.1	Federal parliamentary state A	Canberra	English, indigenous
Australian Capital Territory	927	303,000	327	Territory (Australia) D	Canberra	English
† Austria	32,377	7,913,000	244	Federal republic A	Vienna (Wien)	German
† Azerbaijan	33,436	7,481,000	224	Republic A	Baku (Bakı)	Azeri, Russian, Armenian
† Bahamas	5,382	270,000	50	Parliamentary state A	Nassau	English, Creole
† Bahrain	267	572,000	2,142	Monarchy A	Al Manāmah	Arabic, English, Farsi, Urdu
† Bangladesh	55,598	115,240,000	2,073	Republic A	Dhaka	Bangla, English
† Barbados	166	260,000	1,566	Parliamentary state A	Bridgetown	English
Beijing (Peking)	6,487	11,365,000	1,752	Autonomous city (China) D	Beijing (Peking)	Chinese (Mandarin)
† Belarus	80,155	10,380,000	129	Republic A	Minsk	Belarussian, Russian
Belau see Palau						
† Belgium	11,783	10,050,000	853	Constitutional monarchy A	Brussels (Bruxelles)	Dutch (Flemish), French, German
† Belize	8,866	205,000	23	Parliamentary state A	Belmopan	English, Spanish, Mayan, Garifuna
† Benin	43,475	5,292,000	122	Republic A	Porto-Novo and Cotonou	French, Fon, Yoruba, indigenous
Bermuda	21	76,000	3,619	Dependent territory (U.K.) C	Hamilton	English
† Bhutan	17,954	1,707,000	95	Monarchy (Indian protection) B	Thimphu	Dzongkha, Tibetan and Nepalese dialects
† Bolivia	424,165	7,582,000	18	Republic A	La Paz and Sucre	Aymara, Quechua, Spanish
† Bosnia and Herzegovina	19,741	4,442,000	225	Republic A	Sarajevo	Serbo-Croatian
† Botswana	224,711	1,424,000	6.3	Republic A	Gaborone	English, Tswana
† Brazil	3,286,500	151,310,000	46	Federal republic A	Brasília	Portuguese, Spanish, English, French
British Columbia	365,948	3,354,000	9.2	Province (Canada) D	Victoria	English
British Indian Ocean Territory	23	(1)		Dependent territory (U.K.) C		English
British Virgin Islands	59	13,000	220	Dependent territory (U.K.) C	Road Town	English
† Brunei	2,226	279,000	125	Monarchy A	Bandar Seri Begawan	Malay, English, Chinese
† Bulgaria	42,855	8,813,000	206	Republic A	Sofia (Sofiya)	Bulgarian, Turkish
† Burkina Faso	105,869	9,922,000	94	Republic A	Ouagadougou	French, indigenous
Burma see Myanmar						
† Burundi	10,745	6,015,000	560	Republic A	Bujumbura	French, Kirundi, Swahili
California	163,707	31,905,000	195	State (U.S.) D	Sacramento	English
† Cambodia	69,898	10,010,000	143	Transitional government A	Phnum Pénh (Phnom Penh)	Khmer, French
† Cameroon	183,568	12,845,000	70	Republic A	Yaoundé	English, French, indigenous
† Canada	3,849,674	27,950,000	7.3	Federal parliamentary state A	Ottawa	English, French
† Cape Verde	1,557	414,000	266	Republic A	Praia	Portuguese, Crioulo
Cayman Islands	100	32,000	320	Dependent territory (U.K.) C	George Town	English
† Central African Republic	240,535	3,089,000	13	Republic A	Bangui	French, Sango, Arabic, indigenous
Ceylon see Sri Lanka						
† Chad	495,755	6,149,000	12	Republic A	N'Djamena	Arabic, French, indigenous
Channel Islands	75	149,000	1,987	Dependent territory (U.K.) B		English, French
† Chile	292,135	13,795,000	47	Republic A	Santiago	Spanish
† China (excl. Taiwan)	3,689,631	1,184,060,000	321	Socialist republic A	Beijing (Peking)	Chinese dialects

Region or Political Division	Area Sq. Mi.	Est. Pop. 1/1/94	Pop. Per. Sq. Mi.	Form of Government and Ruling Power		Capital	Predominant Languages
Christmas Island	52	1,300	25	External territory (Australia)	C	The Settlement	English, Chinese, Malay
Cocos (Keeling) Islands	5.4	600	111	Territory (Australia)	C	West Island	English, Cocos-Malay, Malay
† Colombia	440,831	35,085,000	80	Republic	A	Bogotá	Spanish
Colorado	104,100	3,528,000	34	State (U.S.)	D	Denver	English
† Comoros (excl. Mayotte)	863	508,000	589	Federal Islamic republic	A	Moroni	Arabic, French, Comoran
† Congo	132,047	2,403,000	18	Republic	A	Brazzaville	French, Lingala, Kikongo, indigenous
Connecticut	5,544	3,272,000	590	State (U.S.)	D	Hartford	English
Cook Islands	91	19,000	209	Self-governing territory (New Zealand protection)	B	Avarua	English, Maori
† Costa Rica	19,730	3,285,000	166	Republic	A	San José	Spanish
† Cote d'Ivoire	124,518	13,930,000	112	Republic	A	Abidjan and Yamoussoukro (⁴)	French, Dioula and other indigenous
† Croatia	21,829	4,796,000	220	Republic	A	Zagreb	Sebo-Croatian
† Cuba	42,804	11,015,000	257	Socialist republic	A	Havana (La Habana)	Spanish
† Cyprus	2,276	574,000	252	Republic	A	Nicosia (Levkosía)	Greek, English
Cyprus, North (²)	1,295	193,000	149	Republic	A	Nicosia (Lefkoşa)	Turkish
† Czech Republic	30,450	10,400,000	342	Republic	A	Prague (Praha)	Czech, Slovak
Delaware	2,489	700,000	281	State (U.S.)	D	Dover	English
† Denmark	16,639	5,181,000	311	Constitutional monarchy	A	Copenhagen (København)	Danish
District of Columbia	68	576,000	8,471	Federal district (U.S.)	D	Washington	English
† Djibouti	8,958	579,000	65	Republic	A	Djibouti	French, Arabic, Somali, Afar
† Dominica	305	87,000	285	Republic	A	Roseau	English, French
† Dominican Republic	18,704	7,715,000	412	Republic	A	Santo Domingo	Spanish
† Ecuador	105,037	10,515,000	100	Republic	A	Quito	Spanish, Quechua, indigenous
† Egypt	386,662	56,820,000	147	Socialist republic	A	Cairo (Al Qāhirah)	Arabic
Ellice Islands see Tuvalu							
† El Salvador	8,124	5,179,000	637	Republic	A	San Salvador	Spanish, Nahua
England	50,352	48,320,000	960	Administrative division (U.K.)	D	London	English
† Equatorial Guinea	10,831	379,000	35	Republic	A	Malabo	Spanish, indigenous, English
† Eritrea	36,170	3,540,000	98	Republic	A	Asmera	Tigre, Kunama, Cushitic dialects, Nora Bana, Arabic
† Estonia	17,413	1,608,000	92	Republic	A	Tallinn	Estonian, Latvian, Lithuanian, Russian
† Ethiopia	446,953	54,170,000	121	Provisional military government	A	Addis Ababa	Amharic, Tigrinya, Orominga, Guaraginga, Somali, Arabic
Europe	3,800,000	709,300,000	187				
Faeroe Islands	540	48,000	89	Self-governing territory (Danish protection)	B	Tórshavn	Danish, Faroese
Falkland Islands (³)	4,700	2,200	0.5	Dependent territory (U.K.)	C	Stanley	English
† Fiji	7,056	759,000	108	Republic	A	Suva	English, Fijian, Hindustani
† Finland	130,559	5,056,000	39	Republic	A	Helsinki (Helsingfors)	Finnish, Swedish, Lapp, Russian
Florida	65,758	13,855,000	211	State (U.S.)	D	Tallahassee	English
† France (excl. Overseas Departments)	211,208	57,680,000	273	Republic	A	Paris	French
French Guiana	35,135	134,000	3.8	Overseas department (France)	C	Cayenne	French
French Polynesia	1,359	211,000	155	Overseas territory (France)	C	Papeete	French, Tahitian
Fujian	46,332	31,375,000	677	Province (China)	D	Fuzhou	Chinese dialects
† Gabon	103,347	1,127,000	11	Republic	A	Libreville	French, Fang, indigenous
† Gambia	4,127	919,000	223	Republic	A	Banjul	English, Malinke, Wolof, Fula, indigenous
Gansu	173,746	23,445,000	135	Province (China)	D	Lanzhou	Chinese (Mandarin), Mongolian, Tibetan dialects
Gaza Strip	146	745,000	5,103	Israeli territory with limited self-government			Arabic
Georgia	59,441	6,875,000	116	State (U.S.)	D	Atlanta	English
† Georgia	26,911	5,646,000	210	Republic	A	Tbilisi	Georgian, Russian, Armenian, Azeri
† Germany	137,822	80,930,000	587	Federal republic	A	Berlin and Bonn	German
† Ghana	92,098	16,595,000	180	Republic	A	Accra	English, Akan and other indigenous
Gibraltar	2.3	32,000	13,913	Dependent territory (U.K.)	C	Gibraltar	English, Spanish, Italian, Portuguese, Russian
Gilbert Islands see Kiribati							
Golan Heights	454	29,000	64	Occupied by Israel			Arabic, Hebrew
Great Britain see United Kingdom							
† Greece	50,949	10,500,000	206	Republic	A	Athens (Athínai)	Greek, English, French
Greenland	840,004	57,000	0.1	Self-governing territory (Danish protection)	B	Godtháb	Danish, Greenlandic, Inuit dialects
† Grenada	133	91,000	684	Parliamentary state	A	St. George's	English, French
Guadeloupe (incl. Dependencies)	687	424,000	617	Overseas department (France)	C	Basse-Terre	French, Creole
Guam	209	147,000	703	Unincorporated territory (U.S.)	C	Agana	English, Chamorro, Japanese
Guangdong	68,726	65,830,000	958	Province (China)	D	Guangzhou (Canton)	Chinese dialects, Miao-Yao
Guangxi Zhuangzu	91,236	44,285,000	485	Autonomous region (China)	D	Nanning	Chinese dialects, Thai, Miao-Yao
† Guatemala	42,042	10,510,000	250	Republic	A	Guatemala	Spanish, Amerindian
Guernsey (incl. Dependencies)	30	63,000	2,100	Crown dependency (U.K. protection)	B	St. Peter Port	English, French
† Guinea	94,926	6,274,000	66	Provisional military government	A	Conakry	French, indigenous
† Guinea-Bissau	13,948	1,078,000	77	Republic	A	Bissau	Portuguese, Crioulo, indigenous
Guizhou	65,637	33,985,000	518	Province (China)	D	Guiyang	Chinese (Mandarin), Thai, Miao-Yao
† Guyana	83,000	732,000	8.8	Republic	A	Georgetown	English, indigenous
Hainan	13,127	6,867,000	523	Province (China)	D	Haikou	Chinese, Min, Tai
† Haiti	10,714	6,411,000	598	Provisional military government	A	Port-au-Prince	Creole, French
Hawaii	10,932	1,167,000	107	State (U.S.)	D	Honolulu	English, Hawaiian, Japanese
Hebei	73,359	63,940,000	872	Province (China)	D	Shijiazhuang	Chinese (Mandarin)
Heilongjiang	181,082	36,945,000	204	Province (China)	D	Harbin	Chinese dialects, Mongolian, Tungus
Henan	64,479	89,520,000	1,388	Province (China)	D	Zhengzhou	Chinese (Mandarin)
Holland see Netherlands							
† Honduras	43,277	5,206,000	120	Republic	A	Tegucigalpa	Spanish, indigenous
Hong Kong	414	5,890,000	14,227	Chinese territory under British administration	C	Victoria (Hong Kong)	Chinese (Cantonese), English, Putonghua
Hubei	72,356	56,480,000	781	Province (China)	D	Wuhan	Chinese dialects
Hunan	81,081	63,580,000	784	Province (China)	D	Changsha	Chinese dialects, Miao-Yao
† Hungary	35,919	10,295,000	287	Republic	A	Budapest	Hungarian
† Iceland	39,769	262,000	6.6	Republic	A	Reykjavík	Icelandic
Idaho	83,574	1,089,000	13	State (U.S.)	D	Boise	English
Illinois	57,918	11,750,000	203	State (U.S.)	D	Springfield	English
† India (incl. part of Jammu and Kashmir)	1,237,062	906,770,000	733	Federal republic	A	New Delhi	English, Hindi, Telugu, Bengali, indigenous
Indiana	36,420	5,733,000	157	State (U.S.)	D	Indianapolis	English
† Indonesia	752,410	198,810,000	264	Republic	A	Jakarta	Bahasa Indonesia (Malay), English, Dutch, indigenous

Region or Political Division	Area Sq. Mi.	Est. Pop. 1/1/94	Pop. Per. Sq. Mi.	Form of Government and Ruling Power	Capital	Predominant Languages
Iowa	56,276	2,827,000	50	State (U.S.) . . . . D	Des Moines	English
† Iran	632,457	63,940,000	101	Islamic republic . . . . A	Tehrān	Farsi, Turkish dialects, Kurdish
† Iraq	169,235	19,335,000	114	Republic . . . . A	Baghdād	Arabic, Kurdish, Assyrian, Armenian
† Ireland	27,137	3,563,000	131	Republic . . . . A	Dublin (Baile Átha Cliath)	English, Irish Gaelic
Isle of Man	221	72,000	326	Crown dependency (U.K. protection) . . . . . B	Douglas	English, Manx Gaelic
† Israel (excl. Occupied Areas)	8,019	4,950,000	617	Republic . . . . A	Jerusalem (Yerushalayim)	Hebrew, Arabic
† Italy	116,324	56,670,000	487	Republic . . . . A	Rome (Roma)	Italian, German, French, Slovene
Ivory Coast see Cote d'Ivoire	. . . . . .	. . . . . .	. . . .	. . . .	. . . .	. . . .
Jamaica	4,244	2,538,000	598	Parliamentary state . . . . A	Kingston	English, Creole
† Japan	145,870	124,840,000	856	Constitutional monarchy . . . . A	Tōkyō	Japanese
Jersey	45	86,000	1,911	Crown dependency (U.K. protection) . . . . . B	St. Helier	English, French
Jiangsu	39,614	70,210,000	1,772	Province (China) . . . . D	Nanjing (Nanking)	Chinese dialects
Jiangxi	64,325	39,550,000	615	Province (China) . . . . D	Nanchang	Chinese dialects
Jilin	72,201	25,815,000	358	Province (China) . . . . D	Changchun	Chinese (Mandarin), Mongolian, Korean
† Jordan	35,135	3,858,000	110	Constitutional monarchy . . . . A	'Ammān	Arabic
Kansas	82,282	2,568,000	31	State (U.S.) . . . . D	Topeka	English
† Kazakhstan	1,049,156	17,190,000	16	Republic . . . . A	Alma-Ata (Almaty) and Akmola (⁴)	Kazakh, Russian
Kentucky	40,411	3,813,000	94	State (U.S.) . . . . D	Frankfort	English
† Kenya	224,961	28,280,000	126	Republic . . . . A	Nairobi	English, Swahili, indigenous
Kiribati	313	77,000	246	Republic . . . . A	Bairiki	English, Gilbertese
† Korea, North	46,540	22,735,000	489	Socialist republic . . . . A	Pyŏngyang	Korean
† Korea, South	38,230	44,250,000	1,157	Republic . . . . A	Seoul (Sŏul)	Korean
† Kuwait	6,880	1,734,000	252	Constitutional monarchy . . . . A	Kuwait	Arabic, English
† Kyrgyzstan	76,641	4,645,000	61	Republic . . . . A	Bishkek	Kirghiz, Russian
† Laos	91,429	4,601,000	50	Socialist republic . . . . A	Viangchan (Vientiane)	Lao, French, English
† Latvia	24,595	2,556,000	104	Republic . . . . A	Rīga	Latvian, Russian, Lithuanian
† Lebanon	4,015	3,566,000	888	Republic . . . . A	Beirut (Bayrūt)	Arabic, French, Armenian, English
† Lesotho	11,720	1,907,000	163	Constitutional monarchy under military rule . . A	Maseru	English, Sesotho, Zulu, Xhosa
Liaoning	56,255	41,325,000	735	Province (China) . . . . D	Shenyang	Chinese (Mandarin), Mongolian
† Liberia	38,250	2,901,000	76	Republic . . . . A	Monrovia	English, indigenous
† Libya	679,362	4,917,000	7.2	Socialist republic . . . . A	Tripoli (Ṭarābulus)	Arabic
† Liechtenstein	62	30,000	484	Constitutional monarchy . . . . A	Vaduz	German
† Lithuania	25,212	3,777,000	150	Republic . . . . A	Vilnius	Lithuanian, Polish, Russian
Louisiana	51,843	4,332,000	84	State (U.S.) . . . . D	Baton Rouge	English
† Luxembourg	998	401,000	402	Constitutional monarchy . . . . A	Luxembourg	French, Luxembourgish, German
Macao	6.6	380,000	57,576	Chinese territory under Portuguese administration C	Macao	Portuguese, Chinese (Cantonese)
† Macedonia	9,928	2,198,000	221	Republic . . . . A	Skopje	Macedonian, Albanian
† Madagascar	226,658	13,110,000	58	Republic . . . . A	Antananarivo	Malagasy, French
Maine	35,387	1,245,000	35	State (U.S.) . . . . D	Augusta	English
† Malawi	45,747	8,942,000	195	Republic . . . . A	Lilongwe	Chichewa, English
† Malaysia	127,320	19,060,000	150	Federal constitutional monarchy . . . . A	Kuala Lumpur	Malay, Chinese dialects, English, Tamil
† Maldives	115	246,000	2,139	Republic . . . . A	Male	Divehi
† Mali	482,077	8,922,000	19	Republic . . . . A	Bamako	French, Bambara, indigenous
† Malta	122	365,000	2,992	Republic . . . . A	Valletta	English, Maltese
Manitoba	250,947	1,118,000	4.5	Province (Canada) . . . . D	Winnipeg	English
† Marshall Islands	70	52,000	743	Republic (U.S. protection) . . . . A	Majuro (island)	English, indigenous, Japanese
Martinique	425	377,000	887	Overseas department (France) C	Fort-de-France	French, Creole
Maryland	12,407	5,006,000	403	State (U.S.) . . . . D	Annapolis	English
Massachusetts	10,555	6,106,000	578	State (U.S.) . . . . D	Boston	English
† Mauritania	395,956	2,142,000	5.4	Republic . . . . A	Nouakchott	Arabic, Pular, Soninke, Wolof
† Mauritius (incl. Dependencies)	788	1,110,000	1,409	Republic . . . . A	Port Louis	English, Creole, Bhojpuri, French, Hindi, Tamil, others
Mayotte (⁵)	144	91,000	632	Territorial collectivity (France) C	Dzaoudzi and Mamoudzou (⁴)	French, Swahili (Mahorian)
† Mexico	759,534	90,870,000	120	Federal republic . . . . A	Mexico City (Ciudad de México)	Spanish, indigenous
Michigan	96,810	9,550,000	99	State (U.S.) . . . . D	Lansing	English
† Micronesia, Federated States of	271	119,000	439	Republic (U.S. protection) . . . . A	Kolonia and Paliker (⁴)	English, indigenous
Midway Islands	2.0	500	250	Unincorporated territory (U.S.) C		English
Minnesota	86,943	4,539,000	52	State (U.S.) . . . . D	St. Paul	English
Mississippi	48,434	2,646,000	55	State (U.S.) . . . . D	Jackson	English
Missouri	69,709	5,266,000	76	State (U.S.) . . . . D	Jefferson City	English
† Moldova	13,012	4,425,000	340	Republic . . . . A	Chişinău (Kishinev)	Romanian (Moldovan), Russian
† Monaco	0.7	31,000	44,286	Constitutional monarchy . . . . A	Monaco	French, English, Italian, Monegasque
† Mongolia	604,829	2,314,000	3.8	Republic . . . . A	Ulan Bator (Ulaanbaatar)	Khalkha Mongol, Turkish dialects, Russian, Chinese
Montana	147,046	830,000	5.6	State (U.S.) . . . . D	Helena	English
Montserrat	39	13,000	333	Dependent territory (U.K.) C	Plymouth	English
† Morocco (excl. Western Sahara)	172,414	28,095,000	163	Constitutional monarchy . . . . A	Rabat	Arabic, Berber dialects, French
† Mozambique	308,642	16,585,000	54	Republic . . . . A	Maputo	Portuguese, indigenous
† Myanmar (Burma)	261,228	43,630,000	167	Provisional military government . . . . A	Yangon (Rangoon)	Burmese, indigenous
† Namibia	318,253	1,555,000	4.9	Republic . . . . A	Windhoek	English, Afrikaans, German, indigenous
Nauru	8.1	10,000	1,235	Republic . . . . A	Yaren District	Nauruan, English
Nebraska	77,358	1,635,000	21	State (U.S.) . . . . D	Lincoln	English
Nei Monggol (Inner Mongolia)	456,759	22,495,000	49	Autonomous region (China) . . . . D	Hohhot	Mongolian
† Nepal	56,827	20,660,000	364	Constitutional monarchy . . . . A	Kathmandu	Nepali, Maithali, Bhojpuri, other indigenous
† Netherlands	16,164	15,320,000	948	Constitutional monarchy . . . . A	Amsterdam and The Hague ('s-Gravenhage)	Dutch
Netherlands Antilles	309	192,000	621	Self-governing territory (Netherlands protection) . . . . B	Willemstad	Dutch, Papiamento, English
Nevada	110,567	1,375,000	12	State (U.S.) . . . . D	Carson City	English
New Brunswick	28,355	755,000	27	Province (Canada) . . . . D	Fredericton	English, French
New Caledonia	7,358	179,000	24	Overseas territory (France) C	Nouméa	French, indigenous
Newfoundland	156,649	587,000	3.7	Province (Canada) . . . . D	St. John's	English
New Hampshire	9,351	1,167,000	125	State (U.S.) . . . . D	Concord	English
New Hebrides see Vanuatu						
New Jersey	8,722	7,915,000	907	State (U.S.) . . . . D	Trenton	English
New Mexico	121,598	1,608,000	13	State (U.S.) . . . . D	Santa Fe	English, Spanish
New South Wales	309,500	6,117,000	20	State (Australia) . . . . D	Sydney	English
New York	54,475	18,375,000	337	State (U.S.) . . . . D	Albany	English
† New Zealand	104,454	3,486,000	33	Parliamentary state . . . . A	Wellington	English, Maori

Region or Political Division	Area Sq. Mi.	Est. Pop. 1/1/94	Pop. Per. Sq. Mi.	Form of Government and Ruling Power	Capital	Predominant Languages
† Nicaragua	50,054	4,267,000	85	Republic .... A	Managua	Spanish, English, indigenous
† Niger	489,191	8,754,000	18	Provisional military government .... A	Niamey	French, Hausa, Djerma, indigenous
† Nigeria	356,669	94,550,000	265	Provisional military government .... A	Lagos and Abuja	English, Hausa, Fulani, Yoruba, Ibo, indigenous
Ningxia Huizu	25,637	4,855,000	189	Autonomous region (China) .... D	Yinchuan	Chinese (Mandarin)
Niue	100	1,900	19	Self-governing territory (New Zealand protection) .... B	Alofi	English, indigenous
Norfolk Island	14	2,700	193	External territory (Australia) C	Kingston	English, Norfolk
North America	9,500,000	444,600,000	47			
North Carolina	53,821	6,955,000	129	State (U.S.) .... D	Raleigh	English
North Dakota	70,704	632,000	8.9	State (U.S.) .... D	Bismarck	English
Northern Ireland	5,461	1,605,000	294	Administrative division (U.K.) .... D	Belfast	English
Northern Mariana Islands	184	49,000	266	Commonwealth (U.S. protection) ...... B	Saipan (island)	English, Chamorro, Carolinian
Northern Territory	519,771	172,000	0.3	Territory (Australia) .... D	Darwin	English, indigenous
Northwest Territories	1,322,910	56,000	0.1	Territory (Canada) .... D	Yellowknife	English, indigenous
† Norway (incl. Svalbard and Jan Mayen)	149,412	4,301,000	29	Constitutional monarchy .... A	Oslo	Norwegian, Lapp, Finnish
Nova Scotia	21,425	922,000	43	Province (Canada) .... D	Halifax	English
Oceania (incl. Australia)	3,300,000	28,000,000	8.5			
Ohio	44,828	11,155,000	249	State (U.S.) .... D	Columbus	English
Oklahoma	69,903	3,242,000	46	State (U.S.) .... D	Oklahoma City	English
† Oman	82,030	1,659,000	20	Monarchy .... A	Muscat	Arabic, English, Baluchi, Urdu, Indian dialects
Ontario	412,581	10,315,000	25	Province (Canada) .... D	Toronto	English
Oregon	98,386	3,009,000	31	State (U.S.) .... D	Salem	English
† Pakistan (incl. part of Jammu and Kashmir)	339,732	126,090,000	371	Federal Islamic republic .... A	Islāmābād	English, Urdu, Punjabi, Sindhi, Pashto
Palau (Belau)	196	16,000	82	Republic .... A	Koror and Melekeok [4]	Angaur, English, Japanese, Palauan, Sonsorolese, Tobi
† Panama	29,157	2,592,000	89	Republic .... A	Panamá	Spanish, English
† Papua New Guinea	178,704	3,989,000	22	Parliamentary state .... A	Port Moresby	English, Motu, Pidgin, indigenous
† Paraguay	157,048	4,297,000	27	Republic .... A	Asunción	Spanish, Guarani
Pennsylvania	46,058	12,145,000	264	State (U.S.) .... D	Harrisburg	English
† Peru	496,225	23,305,000	47	Republic .... A	Lima	Quechua, Spanish, Aymara
† Philippines	115,831	66,190,000	571	Republic .... A	Manila	English, Pilipino, Tagalog
Pitcairn (incl. Dependencies)	19	100	5.3	Dependent territory (U.K.) C	Adamstown	English, Tahitian
† Poland	121,196	38,540,000	318	Republic .... A	Warsaw (Warszawa)	Polish
† Portugal	35,516	9,961,000	280	Republic .... A	Lisbon (Lisboa)	Portuguese
Prince Edward Island	2,185	140,000	64	Province (Canada) .... D	Charlottetown	English
Puerto Rico	3,515	3,801,000	1,081	Commonwealth (U.S. protection) ...... B	San Juan	Spanish, English
† Qatar	4,412	502,000	114	Monarchy .... A	Doha	Arabic, English
Qinghai	277,994	4,618,000	17	Province (China) .... D	Xining	Tibetan dialects, Mongolian, Turkish dialects, Chinese (Mandarin)
Quebec	594,860	7,070,000	12	Province (Canada) .... D	Québec	French, English
Queensland	666,876	3,111,000	4.7	State (Australia) .... D	Brisbane	English
Reunion	969	643,000	664	Overseas department (France) C	Saint-Denis	French, Creole
Rhode Island	1,545	1,012,000	655	State (U.S.) .... D	Providence	English
Rhodesia see Zimbabwe						
† Romania	91,699	22,770,000	248	Republic .... A	Bucharest (Bucureşti)	Romanian, Hungarian, German
† Russia	6,592,849	150,500,000	23	Federal republic .... A	Moscow (Moskva)	Russian, Tatar, Ukrainian
† Rwanda	10,169	8,196,000	806	Republic .... A	Kigali	French, Kinyarwanda, Kiswahili
St. Helena (incl. Dependencies)	121	7,000	58	Dependent territory (U.K.) C	Jamestown	English
† St. Kitts and Nevis	104	45,000	433	Parliamentary state .... A	Basseterre	English
† St. Lucia	238	151,000	634	Parliamentary state .... A	Castries	English, French
St. Pierre and Miquelon	93	7,000	75	Territorial collectivity (France) C	Saint-Pierre	French
† St. Vincent and the Grenadines	150	115,000	767	Parliamentary state .... A	Kingstown	English, French
† San Marino	24	24,000	1,000	Republic .... A	San Marino	Italian
† Sao Tome and Principe	372	125,000	336	Republic .... A	São Tomé	Portuguese, Fang
Saskatchewan	251,866	1,006,000	4.0	Province (Canada) .... D	Regina	English
† Saudi Arabia	830,000	16,585,000	20	Monarchy .... A	Riyadh (Ar Riyāḍ)	Arabic
Scotland	30,421	5,130,000	169	Administrative division (U.K.) .... D	Edinburgh	English, Scots Gaelic
† Senegal	75,951	8,522,000	112	Republic .... A	Dakar	French, Wolof, Fulani, Serer, indigenous
† Seychelles	175	72,000	411	Republic .... A	Victoria	English, French, Creole
Shaanxi	79,151	34,455,000	435	Province (China) .... D	Xi'an (Sian)	Chinese (Mandarin)
Shandong	59,074	88,450,000	1,497	Province (China) .... D	Jinan	Chinese (Mandarin)
Shanghai	2,394	13,970,000	5,835	Autonomous city (China) .... D	Shanghai	Chinese (Wu)
Shanxi	60,232	30,075,000	499	Province (China) .... D	Taiyuan	Chinese (Mandarin)
Sichuan	220,078	112,250,000	510	Province (China) .... D	Chengdu	Chinese (Mandarin), Tibetan dialects, Miao-Yao
† Sierra Leone	27,925	4,538,000	163	Transitional military government ...... A	Freetown	English, Krio, Mende, Temne, indigenous
† Singapore	246	2,834,000	11,520	Republic .... A	Singapore	Chinese (Mandarin), English, Malay, Tamil
† Slovakia	18,933	5,342,000	282	Republic .... A	Bratislava	Slovak, Hungarian
† Slovenia	7,820	1,986,000	254	Republic .... A	Ljubljana	Slovenian, Serbo-Croatian
† Solomon Islands	10,954	376,000	34	Parliamentary state .... A	Honiara	English, indigenous
† Somalia	246,201	6,541,000	27	None .... A	Mogadishu (Muqdisho)	Arabic, Somali, English, Italian
† South Africa	471,010	42,320,000	90	Republic .... A	Pretoria, Cape Town, and Bloemfontein	Afrikaans, English, Xhosa, Zulu, other indigenous
South America	6,900,000	304,500,000	44			
South Australia	379,925	1,495,000	3.9	State (Australia) .... D	Adelaide	English
South Carolina	32,007	3,657,000	114	State (U.S.) .... D	Columbia	English
South Dakota	77,121	726,000	9.4	State (U.S.) .... D	Pierre	English
South Georgia (incl. Dependencies)	1,450	(1)		Dependent territory (U.K.) C	Grytviken Harbour	English
South West Africa see Namibia						
† Spain	194,885	38,640,000	198	Constitutional monarchy .... A	Madrid	Spanish (Castilian), Catalan, Galician, Basque
Spanish North Africa [6]	12	142,000	11,833	Five possessions (Spain) C		Spanish, Arabic, Berber dialects
Spanish Sahara see Western Sahara						
† Sri Lanka	24,962	17,970,000	720	Socialist republic .... A	Colombo and Sri Jayawardenapura	English, Sinhala, Tamil
† Sudan	967,500	28,900,000	30	Provisional military government .... A	Khartoum (Al Kharṭūm)	Arabic, Nubian and other indigenous, English
† Suriname	63,251	418,000	6.6	Republic .... A	Paramaribo	Dutch, Sranan Tongo, English, Hindustani, Javanese
† Swaziland	6,704	854,000	127	Monarchy .... A	Mbabane and Lobamba	English, siSwati
† Sweden	173,732	8,747,000	50	Constitutional monarchy .... A	Stockholm	Swedish, Lapp, Finnish

Region or Political Division	Area Sq. Mi.	Est. Pop. 1/1/94	Pop. Per. Sq. Mi.	Form of Government and Ruling Power	Capital	Predominant Languages
Switzerland	15,943	7,001,000	439	Federal republic .... A	Bern (Berne)	German, French, Italian, Romansch
† Syria	71,498	13,695,000	192	Socialist republic .... A	Damascus (Dimashq)	Arabic, Kurdish, Armenian, Aramaic, Circassian
Taiwan	13,900	20,945,000	1,507	Republic .... A	T'aipei	Chinese (Mandarin), Taiwanese (Min), Hakka
† Tajikistan	55,251	5,720,000	104	Republic .... A	Dushanbe	Tajik, Uzbek, Russian
† Tanzania	364,900	27,450,000	75	Republic .... A	Dar es Salaam and Dodoma	English, Swahili, indigenous
Tasmania	26,178	483,000	18	State (Australia) .... D	Hobart	English
Tennessee	42,146	5,058,000	120	State (U.S.) .... D	Nashville	English
Texas	268,601	17,925,000	67	State (U.S.) .... D	Austin	English, Spanish
† Thailand	198,115	58,960,000	298	Constitutional monarchy .... A	Bangkok (Krung Thep)	Thai, indigenous
Tianjin (Tientsin)	4,363	9,235,000	2,117	Autonomous city (China) .... D	Tianjin (Tientsin)	Chinese (Mandarin)
† Togo	21,925	4,142,000	189	Provisional military government .... A	Lomé	French, Ewe, Mina, Kabye, Dagomba
Tokelau	4.6	1,500	326	Island territory (New Zealand) C		English, Tokelauan
Tonga	288	104,000	361	Constitutional monarchy .... A	Nuku'alofa	Tongan, English
† Trinidad and Tobago	1,980	1,288,000	651	Republic .... A	Port of Spain	English, Hindi, French, Spanish
Tristan da Cunha	40	300	7.5	Dependency (St. Helena) C	Edinburgh	English
† Tunisia	63,170	8,605,000	136	Republic .... A	Tunis	Arabic, French
† Turkey	300,948	61,540,000	204	Republic .... A	Ankara	Turkish, Kurdish, Arabic
† Turkmenistan	188,456	3,935,000	21	Republic .... A	Ashkhabad	Turkmen, Russian, Uzbek
Turks and Caicos Islands	193	13,000	67	Dependent territory (U.K.) C	Grand Turk	English
Tuvalu	10	10,000	1,000	Parliamentary state .... A	Funafuti	Tuvaluan, English
† Uganda	93,104	18,425,000	198	Republic .... A	Kampala	English, Luganda, Swahili, indigenous
† Ukraine	233,090	52,240,000	224	Republic .... A	Kiev (Kyyiv)	Ukrainian, Russian, Romanian, Polish
† United Arab Emirates	32,278	2,692,000	83	Federation of monarchs .... A	Abū Ẓaby (Abu Dhabi)	Arabic, Farsi, English, Hindi, Urdu
† United Kingdom	94,249	57,960,000	615	Parliamentary monarchy .... A	London	English, Welsh, Scots Gaelic
† United States	3,787,425	259,390,000	68	Federal republic .... A	Washington	English, Spanish
Upper Volta see Burkina Faso	......	....	......	....	......	
† Uruguay	68,500	3,181,000	46	Republic .... A	Montevideo	Spanish
Utah	84,904	1,842,000	22	State (U.S.) .... D	Salt Lake City	English
† Uzbekistan	172,742	22,240,000	129	Republic .... A	Tashkent	Uzbek, Russian
† Vanuatu	4,707	160,000	34	Republic .... A	Port-Vila	Bislama, English, French
Vatican City	0.2	900	4,500	Monarchical-sacerdotal state .... A	Vatican City	Italian, Latin, other
† Venezuela	352,145	20,460,000	58	Federal republic .... A	Caracas	Spanish, Amerindian
Vermont	9,615	585,000	61	State (U.S.) .... D	Montpelier	English
Victoria	87,877	4,566,000	52	State (Australia) .... D	Melbourne	English
† Vietnam	127,428	72,080,000	566	Socialist republic .... A	Hanoi	Vietnamese, French, Chinese, English, Khmer, indigenous
Virginia	42,769	6,485,000	152	State (U.S.) .... D	Richmond	English
Virgin Islands (U.S.)	133	97,000	729	Unincorporated territory (U.S.) C	Charlotte Amalie	English, Spanish, Creole
Wake Island	3.0	300	100	Unincorporated territory (U.S.) C		English
Wales	8,015	2,905,000	362	Administrative division (U.K.) .... D	Cardiff	English, Welsh Gaelic
Wallis and Futuna	98	14,000	143	Overseas territory (France) C	Mata-Utu	French, Wallisian
Washington	71,303	5,188,000	73	State (U.S.) .... D	Olympia	English
West Bank (incl. Jericho and East Jerusalem)	2,347	1,460,000	622	Israeli territory with limited self-government		Arabic, Hebrew
Western Australia	975,101	1,703,000	1.7	State (Australia) .... D	Perth	English
Western Sahara	102,703	208,000	2.0	Occupied by Morocco C		Arabic
† Western Samoa	1,093	168,000	154	Constitutional monarchy .... A	Apia	English, Samoan
West Virginia	24,231	1,816,000	75	State (U.S.) .... D	Charleston	English
Wisconsin	65,503	5,058,000	77	State (U.S.) .... D	Madison	English
Wyoming	97,818	467,000	4.8	State (U.S.) .... D	Cheyenne	English
Xinjiang Uygur (Sinkiang)	617,764	15,865,000	26	Autonomous region (China) .... D	Ürümqi	Turkish dialects, Mongolian, Tungus, English
Xizang (Tibet)	471,045	2,250,000	4.8	Autonomous region (China) .... D	Lhasa	Tibetan dialects
† Yemen	203,850	10,840,000	53	Republic .... A	San'a'	Arabic
Yugoslavia	39,449	10,730,000	272	Republic .... A	Belgrade (Beograd)	Serbo-Croatian 95%, Albanian 5%
Yukon Territory	186,661	28,000	0.2	Territory (Canada) .... D	Whitehorse	English, Inuktitut, indigenous
Yunnan	152,124	38,720,000	255	Province (China) .... D	Kunming	Chinese (Mandarin), Tibetan dialects, Khmer, Miao-Yao
† Zaire	905,446	41,675,000	46	Republic .... A	Kinshasa	French, Kikongo, Lingala, Swahili, Tshiluba, Kingwana
† Zambia	290,586	8,625,000	30	Republic .... A	Lusaka	English, Tonga, Lozi, other indigenous
Zhejiang	39,305	43,455,000	1,106	Province (China) .... D	Hangzhou	Chinese dialects
† Zimbabwe	150,873	10,605,000	70	Republic .... A	Harare (Salisbury)	English, Shona, Sindebele
WORLD	57,900,000	5,556,000,000	96	....		

† Member of the United Nations
... None, or not applicable.
(1) No permanent population.
(2) North Cyprus unilaterally declared its independence from Cyprus in 1983.
(3) Claimed by Argentina.
(4) Future capital.
(5) Claimed by Comoros.
(6) Comprises Ceuta, Melilla, and several small islands.

Map Symbols

In a very real sense, the whole map is a symbol, representing the world or a part of it. It is a reduced representation of the earth; each of the world's features—cities rivers, etc.—is represented on the map by a symbol. Map symbols may take the form of points, such as dots or squares (often used for cities, capital cities, or points of interest), or lines (roads, railroads, rivers). Symbols may also occupy an area, showing extent of coverage (terrain, forests, deserts). They seldom look like the feature they represent and therefore must be identified and interpreted. For instance, the maps in this atlas define political units by colored tints. Neither the colors nor the boundary lines are actually found on the surface of the earth, but because countries and states are such important political components of the world, strong symbols are used to represent them. On the maps in this atlas the surface configuration of the earth is represented by hill-shading, which gives the three-dimensional impression of landforms. This terrain representation conveys a realistic and readily visualized impression of the surface. A complete legend to the right provides a key to the other symbols on the maps in this atlas.

In this atlas a "local-name" policy generally was used for naming cities and towns and all local topographic and water features. However, for a few major cities the Anglicized name was preferred and the local name given in parentheses, for instance, Moscow (Moskva), Vienna (Wien), Prague (Praha). In countries where more than one official language is used, a name is in the dominant local language. The generic parts of local names for topographic and water features are self-explanatory in many cases because of the associated map symbols or type styles.

Cultural Features

Political Boundaries

International

Secondary: State, Provincial, etc.
(Second order political unit)

Disputed de jure

Cities, Towns and Villages
(Note: On maps at 1:45,000,000 and smaller the town symbols do not follow the specific population classification shown below.)

PARIS — 1,000,000 and over

Milwaukee — 250,000 to 1,000,000

Huntsville — 100,000 to 250,000

Bloomington — 25,000 to 100,000

New Meadows — 0 to 25,000

BUDAPEST — National Capitals

Springfield — Secondary Capitals

Other Cultural Features

Research Stations

Ruins

Transportation

Primary Roads

Secondary Roads

Railroads

Topographic Features

Nev. Sajama 21,463 — Peaks
Elevations are given in feet

Water Features

Lakes and Reservoirs

Fresh Water

Fresh Water: Intermittent

Salt Water

Other Water Features

Rivers

Rivers: Intermittent

Reefs

Ice Shelf

Scale 1:100,000,000; one inch to 1578 miles
Robinson Projection

| 0 | 400 | 800 | 1200 | 1600 | 2000 Miles |

| 0 | 600 | 1200 | 1800 | 2400 | 3000 Kilometers |

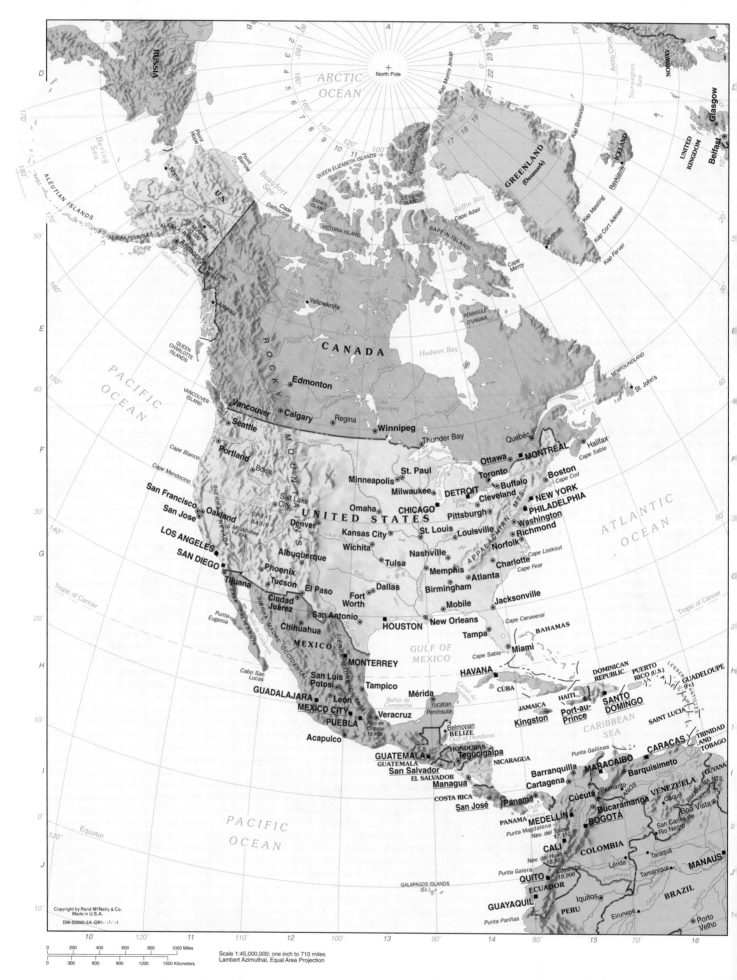

ARCTIC OCEAN

North Pole

RUSSIA

GREENLAND (Denmark)

NORWAY

Noruegian Sea

ICELAND

Reykjavik

UNITED KINGDOM

Belfast

Glasgow

ARCTIC Circle

Kap Morris Jesup

Kap Brewster

ELLESMERE ISLAND

QUEEN ELIZABETH ISLANDS

Kap Meating

Kap Cort Adelaer

Beaufort Sea

BANKS ISLAND

DEVON ISLAND

Baffin Bay

Cape Adair

BAFFIN ISLAND

Kap Farvel

Godthåb

Cape Mercy

Point Hope

Point Barrow

ALEUTIAN ISLANDS

Bering Sea

Nome

Fairbanks

U.S.

ALASKA RANGE

Mt. McKinley

ALASKA PENINSULA

Gulf of Alaska

Anchorage

Mt. Logan 19,551

Juneau

Yellowknife

Great Bear Lake

Great Slave Lake

CANADA

Hudson Bay

PÉNINSULE D'UNGAVA

PACIFIC OCEAN

QUEEN CHARLOTTE ISLANDS

VANCOUVER ISLAND

ROCKY MOUNTAINS

Edmonton

Vancouver

Calgary

Seattle

Regina

Winnipeg

Thunder Bay

Lake Superior

NEWFOUNDLAND

St. John's

Québec

Halifax

Cape Sable

Gulf of St. Lawrence

Cape Blanco

Cape Mendocino

Portland

Boise

Columbia

Missouri

SIERRA NEVADA

San Francisco

Oakland

San Jose

Salt Lake City

GREAT BASIN

Denver

UNITED STATES

Omaha

Minneapolis

Milwaukee

St. Paul

CHICAGO

Lake Michigan

DETROIT

Lake Huron

Ottawa

Toronto

Lake Ontario

MONTRÉAL

Boston

Cape Cod

Buffalo

Cleveland

NEW YORK

Lake Erie

PHILADELPHIA

Pittsburgh

APPALACHIAN MTS.

Washington

Richmond

ATLANTIC OCEAN

LOS ANGELES

SAN DIEGO

Mt. Whitney 14,494

Albuquerque

Phoenix

Tucson

Kansas City

Wichita

St. Louis

Tulsa

Memphis

Nashville

Louisville

Norfolk

Charlotte

Cape Lookout

Cape Fear

Tijuana

El Paso

Ciudad Juárez

Dallas

Fort Worth

Birmingham

Atlanta

Mobile

Jacksonville

Chihuahua

San Antonio

HOUSTON

New Orleans

Cape Canaveral

BRAJA CALIFORNIA

Punta Eugenia

SIERRA MADRE OCCIDENTAL

MEXICO

Golfo de California

MONTERREY

San Luis Potosí

Tampico

Tampa

GULF OF MEXICO

Cape Sable

Miami

BAHAMAS

Cabo San Lucas

GUADALAJARA

León

MEXICO CITY

Veracruz

Mérida

Yucatan Peninsula

Bahía de Campeche

Canal de Yucatán

HAVANA

CUBA

JAMAICA

Kingston

HAITI

Port-au-Prince

DOMINICAN REPUBLIC

SANTO DOMINGO

PUERTO RICO (U.S.)

GUADELOUPE (Fr.)

SAINT LUCIA

LESSER ANTILLES

PUEBLA

Pico de Orizaba 18,406

Acapulco

Belmopan

BELIZE

GUATEMALA

GUATEMALA

San Salvador

EL SALVADOR

Gulf of Honduras

HONDURAS

Tegucigalpa

Managua

NICARAGUA

Lake Nicaragua

COSTA RICA

San José

Golfo de Panamá

PANAMA

Panama

Punta Gallinas

Barranquilla

Cartagena

MARACAIBO

Cúcuta

Bucaramanga

Palmarito

Barquisimeto

VENEZUELA

CARACAS

TRINIDAD AND TOBAGO

GUYANA

CARIBBEAN SEA

PACIFIC OCEAN

Equator

GALAPAGOS ISLANDS (Ec.)

MEDELLÍN

BOGOTÁ

CALI

COLOMBIA

Punta Magdalena

Nev. del Tolima 17,110

Nev. del Huila 18,865

Cayambe 18,996

QUITO

ECUADOR

GUAYAQUIL

PERU

Iquitos

Eirunepé

Punta Pariñas

San Carlos de Río Negro

Boa Vista

PAKARAIMA MTS.

LLANOS

Tamanaquá

Taraquá

Lérida

MANAUS

BRAZIL

Porto Velho

Tropic of Cancer

10	200	400	600	800	1000 Miles

0	300	600	900	1200	1500 Kilometers

Scale 1:45,000,000; one inch to 710 miles
Lambert Azimuthal, Equal Area Projection

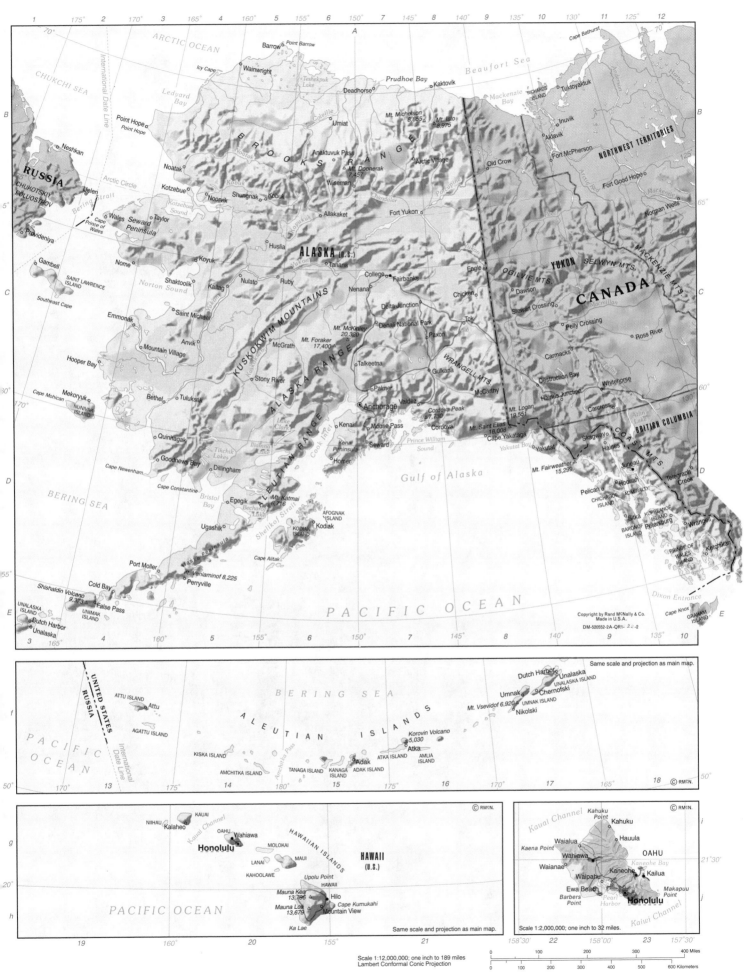

Main map (Alaska and Canada)

ARCTIC OCEAN

CHUKCHI SEA

International Date Line

Ledyard Bay

Beaufort Sea

Barrow · Point Barrow
Icy Cape
Wainwright
Teshekpuk Lake
Prudhoe Bay · Kaktovik
Deadhorse
Cape Bathurst
Mackenzie Bay
RICHARDS ISLAND
Tuktoyaktuk

Point Hope
Point Hope

Neshkan

RUSSIA

CHUKOTSKIY POLUOSTROV

Uelen

Arctic Circle

Bering Strait

Cape Prince of Wales

Providentiya

Wales
Seward Peninsula
Taylor

Noatak
Kobuk
Shungnak Kobuk
Kotzebue
Kotzebue Sound
Noorvik

BROOKS RANGE

Mt. Michelson 8,855
Mt. Isto 8,975

Anaktuvuk Pass
Mt. Doonerak 7,457
Arctic Village

Old Crow

Inuvik
Aklavik
Fort McPherson

NORTHWEST TERRITORIES

Fort Good Hope

Norman Wells

Mackenzie

Umiat

Wiseman

Allakaket

Fort Yukon

Chandalar

Porcupine

Huslia

ALASKA (U.S.)

Gambell
SAINT LAWRENCE ISLAND
Southeast Cape

Nome
Koyuk
Shaktoolik
Kaltag
Nulato
Ruby
Tanana

College · Fairbanks
Nenana

Eagle

Dawson

YUKON
OGILVIE MTS.
SELWYN MTS.
MACKENZIE MTS.

CANADA

Saint Michael

Emmonak
Anvik
Mountain Village

McGrath

KUSKOKWIM MOUNTAINS

Mt. McKinley 20,320
Mt. Foraker 17,400

Delta Junction
Denali National Park

Chicken

Stewart Crossing

Pelly Crossing

Carmacks

Ross River

Hooper Bay

Mekoryuk
NUNIVAK ISLAND

Cape Mohican

Bethel
Tuluksak

Stony River

Lake Clark

Talkeetna

Palmer

Gulkana

Paxon

Tok

WRANGELL MTS.

McCarthy

Destruction Bay

Whitehorse

Haines Junction

Quinhagak

Goodnews Bay
Dillingham

Tikchik Lakes

Iliamna

Anchorage

Kenai
Moose Pass
Cook Inlet

Cordova Peak 7,730
Cordova

Mt. Logan 19,551

Carcross

Skagway
Haines

BRITISH COLUMBIA

COAST MTS.

Cape Newenham
Cape Constantine

Bristol Bay

Egegik
Becharof Lake

LEUTIAN RANGE

ALASKA RANGE

Kenai Peninsula
Homer
Seward

Prince William Sound

Mt. Saint Elias 18,008
Cape Yakataga

Yakutat Bay
Yakutat

Juneau

Telegraph Creek

BERING SEA

Ugashik

Mt. Katmai 6,716

AFOGNAK ISLAND
KODIAK ISLAND
Kodiak

Gulf of Alaska

Mt. Fairweather 15,299

Pelican
Hoonah
CHICHAGOF ISLAND
ADMIRALTY ISLAND

Sitka
BARONOF ISLAND
KUPREANOF ISLAND
Petersburg
Wrangell

Port Moller

Cold Bay

Shishaldin Volcano 9,373
False Pass

Perryville
Mt. Veniaminof 8,225

Cape Alitak

PACIFIC OCEAN

PRINCE OF WALES ISLAND
Ketchikan

UNALASKA ISLAND
Dutch Harbor
Unalaska
UNIMAK ISLAND

Copyright by Rand McNally & Co.
Made in U.S.A.
DM-520552-2A-QR1- 2 2 -2

Dixon Entrance
Cape Knox
GRAHAM ISLAND

Aleutian Islands inset

Same scale and projection as main map.

UNITED STATES
RUSSIA
International Date Line

PACIFIC OCEAN

BERING SEA

ATTU ISLAND
Attu
AGATTU ISLAND

ALEUTIAN ISLANDS

KISKA ISLAND

AMCHITKA ISLAND
Amchitka Pass
TANAGA ISLAND
KANAGA ISLAND
Adak
ADAK ISLAND
ATKA ISLAND
Korovin Volcano 5,030
Atka
AMLIA ISLAND

Mt. Vsevidof 6,920
UMNAK ISLAND
Nikolski

Umnak
Chernofski
Dutch Harbor
Unalaska
UNALASKA ISLAND

© RMcN.

Hawaii inset (left)

© RMcN.

NIIHAU
Kalaheo
KAUAI

Kauai Channel

OAHU
Wahiawa
Honolulu
MOLOKAI
LANAI
MAUI
KAHOOLAWE

HAWAIIAN ISLANDS

HAWAII (U.S.)

Upolu Point
HAWAII
Mauna Kea 13,796
Hilo
Cape Kumukahi
Mauna Loa 13,679
Mountain View
Ka Lae

PACIFIC OCEAN

Same scale and projection as main map.

Oahu inset (right)

© RMcN.

Kauai Channel
Kahuku Point
Kahuku
Waialua
Hauula
Kaena Point
Wahiawa
OAHU
Waianae
Waipahu
Kaneohe Bay
Kaneohe
Kailua
Ewa Beach
Barbers Point
Pearl Harbor
Honolulu
Makapuu Point
Kaiwi Channel

Scale 1:2,000,000; one inch to 32 miles.

Scale 1:12,000,000; one inch to 189 miles
Lambert Conformal Conic Projection

0 100 200 300 400 Miles
0 100 200 300 400 500 600 Kilometers

Scale 1:16,000,000; one inch to 252 miles
Lambert Azimuthal, Equal Area Projection

0   100   200   300   400   500 Miles

0   200   400   600   800 Kilometers

Scale 1:12,000,000; one inch to 189 miles
Alber's Conic Equal Area Projection

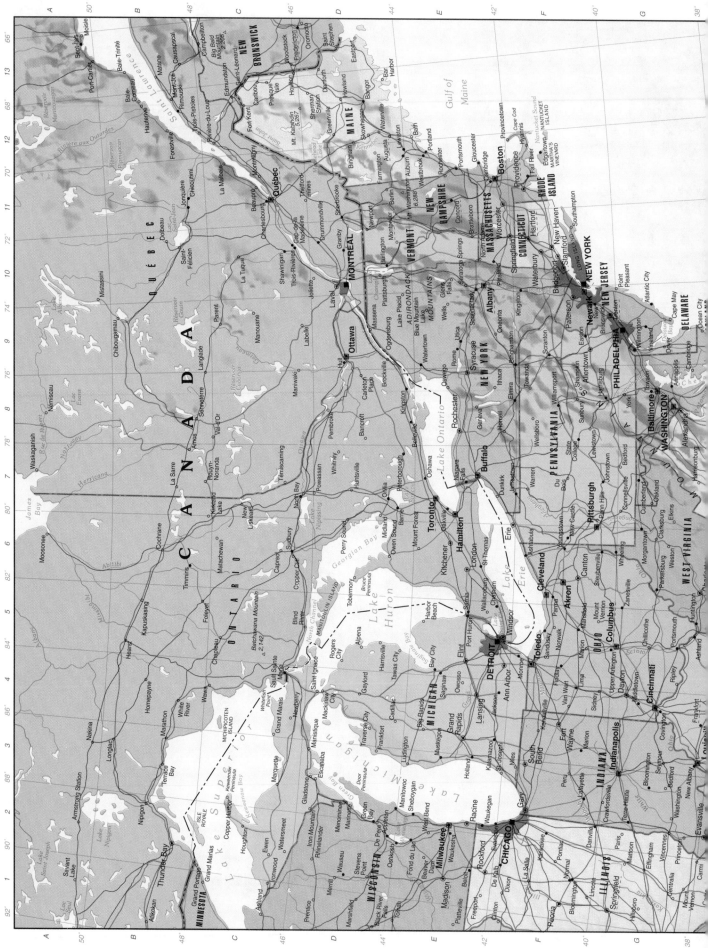

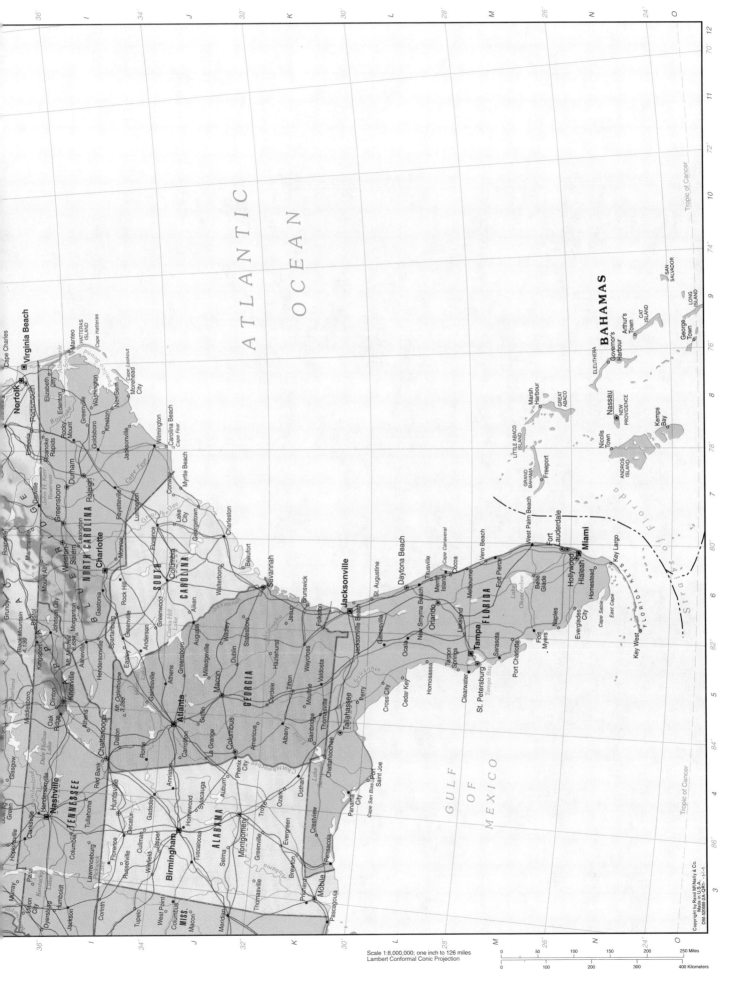

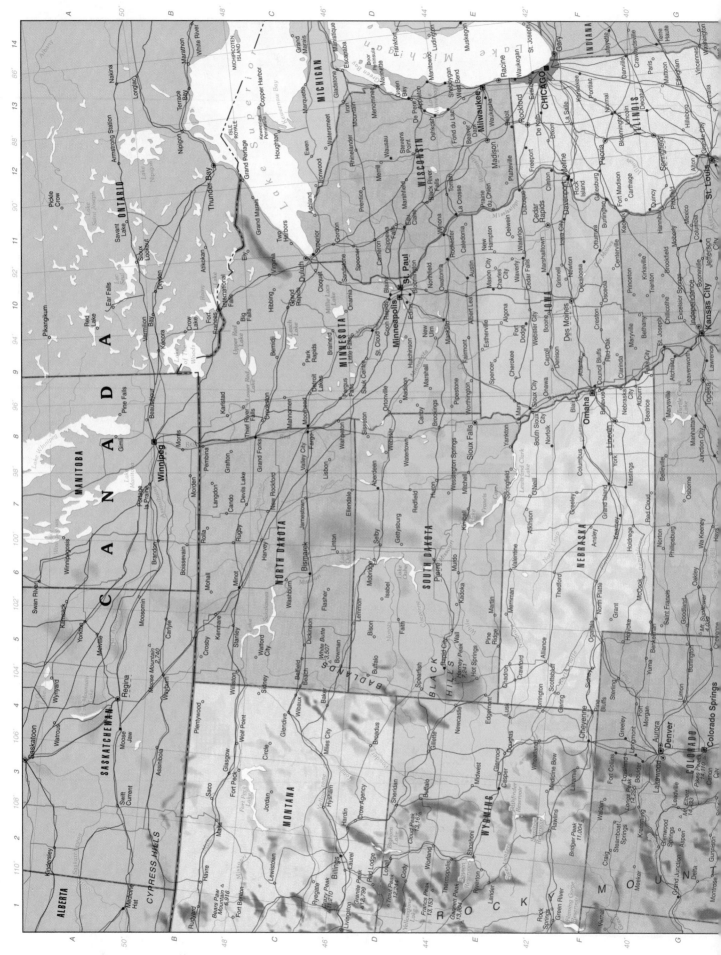

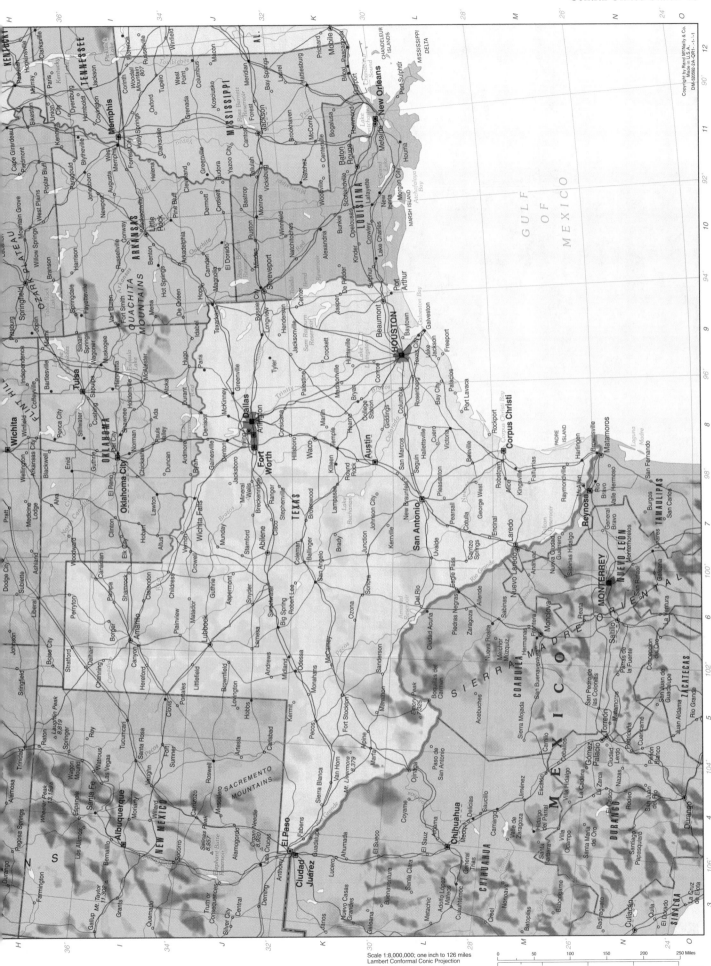

Scale 1:8,000,000; one inch to 126 miles
Lambert Conformal Conic Projection

| 0 | 50 | 100 | 150 | 200 | 250 Miles |

| 0 | 100 | 200 | 300 | 400 Kilometers |

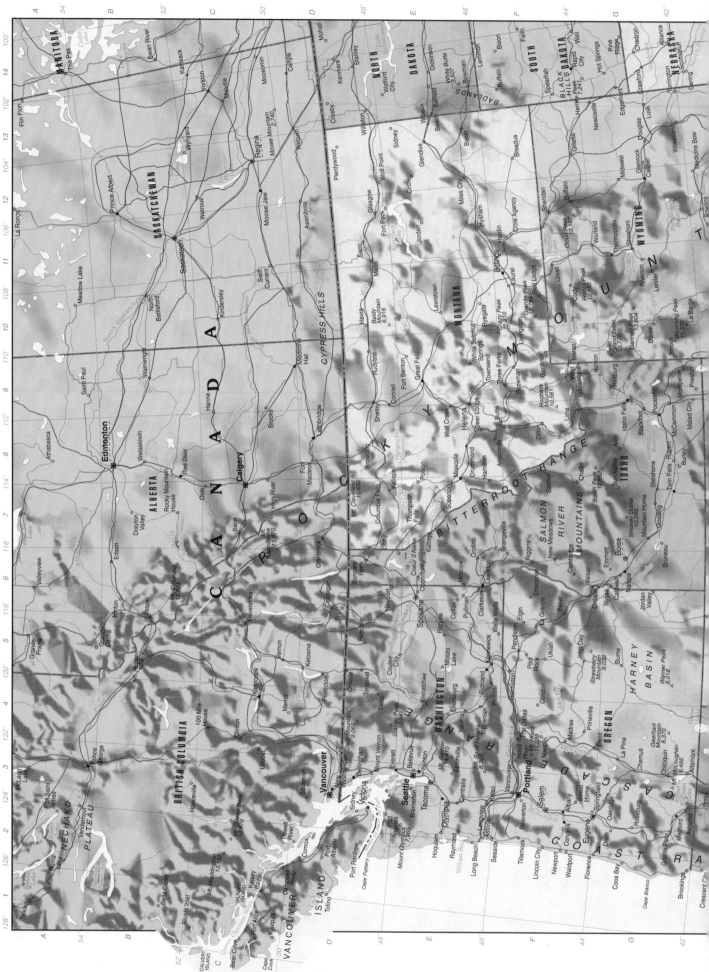

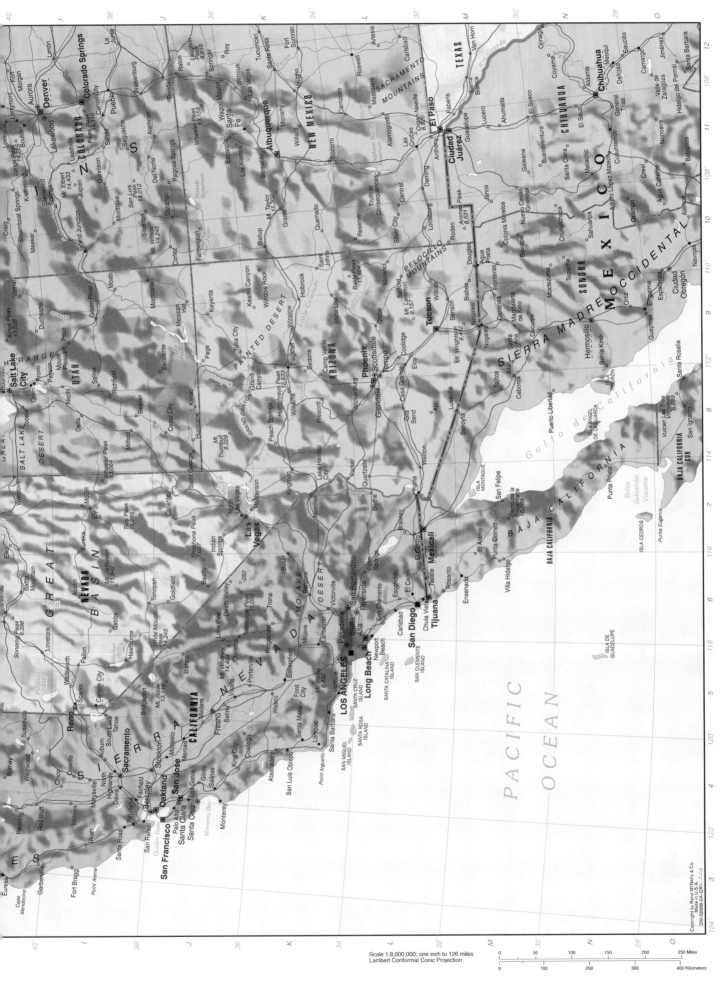

Scale 1:8,000,000; one inch to 126 miles
Lambert Conformal Conic Projection

0	50	100	150	200	250 Miles

0	100	200	300	400 Kilometers

ATLANTIC OCEAN

CARIBBEAN SEA

Scale 1:16,000,000; one inch to 252 miles
Lambert Conformal Conic Projection

PACIFIC OCEAN

Golfo de California

BAJA CALIFORNIA

BAJA CALIFORNIA SUR

ARIZONA

NEW MEXICO

SONORA

CHIHUAHUA

SINALOA

DURANGO

COAHU

ZACATECAS

NAYARIT

JALISCO

COLIMA

MEX

Tropic of Cancer

Tijuana
Ensenada
Mexicali
El Centro
Chula Vista
Tecate
Yuma
Gila Bend
Casa Grande
Coolidge
Eloy
Tucson
Benson
Willcox
El Paso
Ciudad Juárez
Roswell
Hobbs
Las Cruces
Deming
Lordsburg
Silver City
Central
Alamogordo
Artesia
Carlsbad

Guadalajara
Mazatlán
Durango
Culiacán
Los Mochis
Ciudad Obregón
Guaymas
Hermosillo

ISLAS REVILLAGIGEDO (Mex.)
ISLA CLARIÓN (Mex.)
ISLA SOCORRO
ISLA SAN BENEDICTO
ISLA ROCA PARTIDA

ISLAS MARÍAS
ISLA MARÍA MADRE
ISLA MARÍA MAGDALENA
ISLA MARÍA CLEOFAS

0 50 100 150 200 250 Miles
0 100 200 300 400 Kilometers

Copyright by Rand McNally & Co.
Made in U.S.A.
DM-540000-2A-QR1-

Scale 1:45,000,000; one inch to 710 miles
Lambert Azimuthal, Equal Area Projection

Scale 1:16,000,000; one inch to 252 miles
Lambert Conformal Conic Projection

0   100   200   300   400   500 Miles

0   200   400   600   800 Kilometers

NICARAGUA

Cabo Santa Elena
Puntarenas
Alajuela   Puerto Limón
San José
San Isidro   Cerro Chirripó
12,530
Volcán Irazú 11,260
COSTA RICA   David   Volcán Barú 11,401
Puerto Armuelles   Aguadulce   ISTMO
Santiago   Chitré
Punta Burica   La Chorrera
Punta Mariato   Punta Mala   Golfo de
ISLA DE COIBA   Panamá
Peninsula
de Azuero
Punta Marzo

ISLA DEL COCO
(Costa Rica)

ISLA DE MALPELO
(Colombia)

Equator

SAN
CRISTOBAL

GALAPAGOS ISLANDS
(ARCHIPIELAGO DE
COLÓN)
(Ecuador)

ARUBA   NETHERLANDS
(Neth.)   ANTILLES
Punta Gallinas   Oranjestad   CURAÇAO   BONAIRE
Cabo de la Vela   Peninsula   Willemstad
Riohacha   de la Guajira   Maicao   Coro
Santa Marta   Pico   Cristóbal Colón   Punta Fijo
Barranquilla   Sabanalarga   Cabo   Puerto Cabello
Cartagena   Soledad   Ciénaga   Valledupar   MARACAIBO   Altagracia
San Jacinto   Machiques   Cabimas   Barquisimeto
San Onofre   Turbaco   Plato   Carora   VALENCIA
Sincelejo   Corozal   El Banco   Valera   Acarigua
Lorica   Sahagún   Ocaña   La Fria   Barinas
Montería   San Marcos   Caucasia   Cúcuta   San Cristóbal
Chigorodó   Barrancabermeja   Bucaramanga   Guasdualito
Turbo   Floridablanca   Palmarito
Riosucio   Puerto Berrío   Pamplona
Barrancabermeja   VENEZUELA

Cabo Corrientes   Quibdó   MEDELLÍN   La Dorada   Duitama
Itagüí   Envigado   Honda   Sogamoso   Yopal
Manizales   Pereira   Nev. del   Tunja
Cartago   Tolima   BOGOTÁ
Armenia   17,110   Villavicencio
Buenaventura   Tuluá   Ibagué
Buga   Espinal   San Martín   COLOMBIA
Punta Magdalena   CALI   Palmira   San José del
Neiva   Guaviare
Nev. del   Inírida
Popayán   Huila 18,865
Tumaco   Pitalito   Florencia
Cabo Manglares   Pasto
Esmeraldas   Ipiales   Ibarra   Vaupés
Punta Galera   Tulcán   Lérida
Cayambe 18,996   Taraqua
Cabo Pasado   QUITO   Putumayo
Chone   Cotopaxi   Apaporis
19,347   ECUADOR
Manta   Ambato
Cabo San Lorenzo   Portoviejo   Chimborazo 20,702
Jipijapa   Riobamba   Napo
Vinces   Iquitos
Babahoyo   Vol. Sangay   Leticia
Punta Santa Elena   Milagro   17,159
GUAYAQUIL   Cañar
Golfo de Guayaquil   Cuenca
ISLA PUNA   Pasaje
Machala   Loja
Tumbes
Marañón

AMAZONAS
Tamaniquá
Tefé

Talara
Punta Pariñas   Moyobamba
Sullana   Yurimaguas   Eirunepé
Piura   Castilla   Chachapoyas
Sechura   Jaén

Lambayeque   Chiclayo
Pacasmayo   Cajamarca   Cruzeiro
Chocope   do Sul   Lábrea
Trujillo   Pucallpa   ACRE
Chimbote   Nev. Huascarán
22,133   Rio Branco
Tingo   Río Branco
María   Ariquemes   RONDÔN
Huaraz   Huánuco   Guajará-
Huarmey   Cerro de Pasco   Mirim
Nevado Yerupajá   PERU
21,765   Orthon   Porto Ve
Pativilca   Tarma
Huacho   La Oroya   Río de las Piedras
Punta Lachay   Chosica   Puerto Heath
Huaral   Huancayo   Puerto
Callao   Vitarte   Maldonado
Lima   Mala   Huancavelica   Machupicchu   Trinidad
Chincha Alta   Ayacucho   Abancay   Cusco
Pisco   Nevado Auzangate 20,945
Bahía de Paracas   Ica   CORDILLERA   Ayavirí
Punta Carreta   DE HUANZO   Juliaca   BOLIVIA
Nazca   Nevado Coropuna   Lago
20,686   Puno   Titicaca   Nev. Illampu
Punta Parada   Nevado Chachani   21,066
19,931   Arequipa   LA PAZ   Cochabamba
Camaná   Volcán Misti 19,101
Volcán Tutupaca   Nev. Illimani   Santa Cruz
Mollendo   19,898   20,741   de la Sierra
Ilo   Moquegua   Oruro
Tacna   Nev.   Sucre
Sajamá   Lago
PACIFIC OCEAN   Arica   21,463   Poopó   Potosí
Pisagua   CHILE   Pozo Almonte
Iquique
General Eu
Tocopilla   Villamontes
Chuquicamata   Cota
Calama   ARGENTINA
Cerro Licancabur
19,409

0   100   200   300   400   500 Miles
0   200   400   600   800 Kilometers

ATLANTIC OCEAN

TRINIDAD AND TOBAGO
of Spain
n Fernando
TRINIDAD

TOBAGO

Morawhanna
Marlborough
Charity
Suddie
Parika
Georgetown
Enmore
Bartica
New Amsterdam
Nieuw Nickerie
Groningen
Nieuw Amsterdam
Paramaribo
Albina
Iracoubo
Sinnamary
Kourou
Saint-Laurent-du-Maroni
Cayenne
Kwakoegron
Saint-Élie
Guisanbourg
Quanary

GUYANA
Mount Roraima 9,432
Lethem
KANUKU MTS.
Brokopondo
Stuumeer
Juliana Top 4,035
Saül

SURINAME
FRENCH GUIANA

ACARAÍ MTS.
TUMUC-HUMAC MOUNTAINS
Cabo Cacipore
AMAPÁ

ILHA DE MARACÁ
Cabo Norte

a Vista
RAIMA MTS.
IMA
KAMOA MTS.

Represa
Balbina

ILHA BAILIQUE
ILHA DO CURUÁ
ILHA JANAUCU
ILHA CAVIANA DE FORA
ILHA MEXIANA
Cabo Maguari

Oriximiná
Faro
Macapá
ILHA GRANDE DO GURUPÁ
ILHA DE MARAJÓ
Soure
Baía de Marajó

Equator

MANAUS
Itacoatiara
Maués
Santarém
Portel
Breves
Cametá
Belém
Capanema
Bragança
Carutapera
Manacapuru
Altamira
Abaetetuba
São Luís
Parnaíba
Camocim
Itapipoca

Amazon
Represa de
Tucuruí
Tucuruí
Pindaré Mirim
Coroatá
Bacabal
Codó
Caxias
Pedreiras
Campo Maior
Sobral
Fortaleza
Maracanaú
Pacajus
Canindé
CEARÁ
Quixadá

Itaituba
Novo
Aripuanã
PARÁ
SERRA DOS CARAJÁS
Marabá
Imperatriz
MARANHÃO
Timon
Teresina
Crateús
Mossoró
Cabo de São Roque

Conceição
SERRA DOS APIACÁS
Nazaré
Tocantinópolis
São João dos Patos
Floriano
Oeiras
Jaguaribe
Igautu
Caicó
RIO GRANDE DO NORTE
Natal

Vilhena
Alta Floresta
Araguaína
Carolina
Balsas
Picos
PIAUÍ
Crato
Juazeiro do Norte
Patos
PARAÍBA
Guarabira
João Pessoa
Campina Grande
Timbaúba
Olinda
RECIFE

SERRA DO NORTE
SERRA DO TOMBADOR
SERRA DOS PARECIS
Diamantino
Conceição da Araguaia
SERRA DO ESTRONDO
SERRA DO PENITENTE
CHAP. DAS MANGABEIRAS
SERRA DO URUÇUI
Represa Boa Esperança
Curupá
Palmas
Porto Nacional
TOCANTINS
Gurupi
Salgueiro
Serra Talhada
Petrolina
Juàzeiro
Paulo Afonso
PERNAMBUCO
Arcoverde
Garanhuns
Palmeira dos Indios
Caruaru
Palmares
ALAGOAS
Maceió
Arapiraca
Penedo
SERGIPE
Aracaju

MATO GROSSO
SERRA FORMOSA
SERRA DO RONCADOR
B R A Z I L
Barreiras
Ibotirama
Senhor do Bonfim
Irecê
Jacobina
Esplanada
Alagoinhas

Cáceres
Cuiabá
PLANALTO DO MATO GROSSO
Porangatu
Santana
Barras
BAHIA
Bom Jesus da Lapa
Itaberaba
Feira de Santana
Camaçari
SALVADOR
Valença

Jaciara
Barra do Garças
Juçara
Formosa
BRASÍLIA
DISTRITO FEDERAL
São Francisco
Guanambi
Brumado
Jequié
Ipiaú
Itabuna
Ilhéus

Rondonópolis
Inhumas
Iporá
Luziânia
Anápolis
Goiânia
Unaí
Montes Claros
Pedra Azul
Vitória da Conquista
Itapetinga

Mineiros
Jataí
Caiapônia
Pontalina
Pires do Rio
Paracatu
Bocaíuva
Pirapora
Januária
Salinas
Almenara
Itaobim
Canavieiras
Belmonte

MATO GROSSO DO SUL
Coxim
Rio Verde de Mato Grosso
Camapuã
Ituiutaba
Araguari
Patos de Minas
Curvelo
Teófilo Otoni
Itamaraju
Ponta da Baleia

Corumbá
Miranda
Aquidauana
Campo Grande
Paranaíba
Campina Verde
Frutal
Uberlândia
Uberaba
Araxá
Sete Lagoas
MINAS GERAIS
Governador Valadares
Nanuque
São Mateus

Três Lagoas
Araçatuba
São José do Rio Preto
Franca
BELO HORIZONTE
Ipatinga
Linhares
Colatina

Bela Vista
Dourados
Presidente Prudente
Tupã
Lins
Araraquara
São Carlos
Poços de Caldas
Lavras
São João del Rei
Três Rios
Ponte Nova
Vitória
Vila Velha
Itaquari
Cachoeiro de Itapemirim

PARAGUAY
Puerto Bahía Negra
Pedro Juan Caballero
Ponta Porã
Marília
Assis
Piracicaba
SÃO PAULO
Campinas
Taubaté
Juiz de Fora
Volta Redonda
RIO DE JANEIRO
Campos
Nova Friburgo
Cabo de São Tomé

Bauru
São José dos Campos
Sorocaba
Santo André
SÃO PAULO
Santos
São Vicente
Nova Iguaçu
Niterói
RIO DE JANEIRO
Tropic of Capricorn

Scale 1:16,000,000; one inch to 252 miles
Lambert Azimuthal, Equal Area Projection

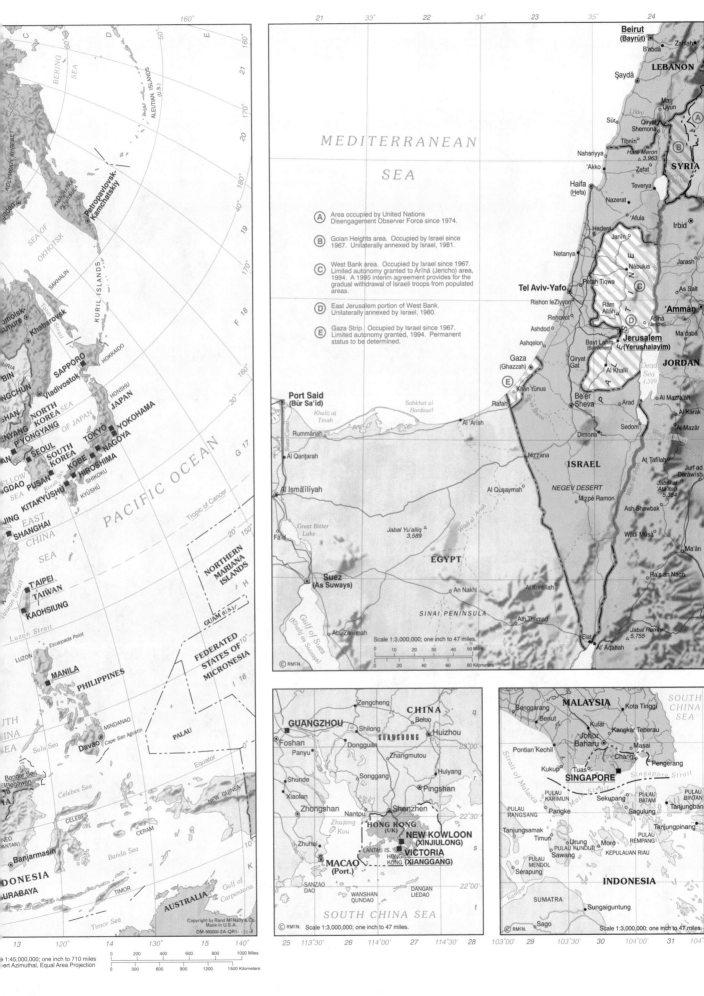

MEDITERRANEAN

SEA

(A) Area occupied by United Nations
Disengagement Observer Force since 1974.

(B) Golan Heights area. Occupied by Israel since
1967. Unilaterally annexed by Israel, 1981.

(C) West Bank area. Occupied by Israel since 1967.
Limited autonomy granted to Arīhā (Jericho) area,
1994. A 1995 interim agreement provides for the
gradual withdrawal of Israeli troops from populated
areas.

(D) East Jerusalem portion of West Bank.
Unilaterally annexed by Israel, 1980.

(E) Gaza Strip. Occupied by Israel since 1967.
Limited autonomy granted, 1994. Permanent
status to be determined.

Beirut
(Bayrūt)
Zahlah
B'abdā
LEBANON
Şaydā
Marj
'Uyūn
Şūr
Qiryat
Shemona
Tibnīn
Hare Meron
△ 3,963
(A)
(B)
SYRIA
Nahariyya
'Akko
Zefat
33°
Haifa
(Hefa)
Teverya
Nazerat
Irbid
'Afula
Hadera
Janīn
Jarash
Netanya
Nābulus
As Salt
Petah Tiqwa
Tel Aviv-Yafo
(C)
Rishon leZiyyon
Rām
Allāh
'Ammān
Rehovot
Arīhā
(Jericho)
Ma'dabā
Ashdod
(D)
Jerusalem
(Yerushalayim)
Ashqelon
Bayt Lahm
(Bethlehem)
JORDAN
Gaza
Qiryat
Gat
Al Khalīl
Dead
Sea
1,339
(Ghazzah)
(E)
Be'er
Sheva
Khān Yūnus
Rāfah
Arad
Al Mazra'ah
Port Said
(Būr Sa'īd)
Sabkhat al
Bardawil
Al 'Arīsh
Sedom
Al Karak
Khalij al
Tinah
Dimona
Al Mazār
Rummānah
Nizzana
At Ţafīlah
Al Qanţarah
ISRAEL
Jurf ad
Darāwīsh
Jabal al
'Atā'iṭah
5,384
Al Ismā'īlīyah
Al Quşaymah
NEGEV DESERT
Mizpé Ramon
Ash Shawbak
Great Bitter
Lake
Jabal Yu'alliq
3,589
Wādī al 'Arīsh
Wādī Mūsā
Fā'id
Ma'ān
EGYPT
Suez
(As Suways)
An Nakhl
Ra's an Naqb
Al Kuntillah
Gulf of Suez
(Khalij as Suways)
SINAI PENINSULA
Ath Thamad
Jabal Ramm
5,755
Abū Zanimah
Elat
Al 'Aqabah

Scale 1:3,000,000; one inch to 47 miles.

© RMcN.

───

CHINA
Zengcheng
GUANGZHOU
Shilong
Beluo
Foshan
GUANGDONG
Huizhou
Panyu
Dongguan
Zhangmutou
Shunde
Songgang
Huiyang
Xiaolan
Zhongshan
Nantou
Pingshan
Zhujiang
Kou
Shenzhen
Zhuhai
HONG KONG
(UK)
NEW KOWLOON
(XINJIULONG)
LANTAU IS.
VICTORIA
HONG
KONG
(XIANGGANG)
MACAO
(Port.)
SANZAO
DAO
WANSHAN
QUNDAO
DANGAN
LIEDAO

© RMcN.   Scale 1:3,000,000; one inch to 47 miles.

SOUTH CHINA SEA

───

SOUTH
CHINA
SEA
Senggarang
MALAYSIA
Kota Tinggi
Benut
Kulai
Kangkar Teberau
Pontian Kechil
Johor
Baharu
Masai
Strait of Malacca
Changi
Pengerang
Kukup
Tuas
SINGAPORE
Singapore Strait
PULAU
KARIMUN
Sekupang
PULAU
BATAM
PULAU
BINTAN
Tanjungban
PULAU
RANGSANG
Pangke
Tanjungpinang
Tanjungsamak
PULAU KUNDUR
Moro
PULAU
REMPANG
Timun
Urung
Sawang
KEPULAUAN RIAU
Serapung
PULAU
MENDOL
Sago
SUMATRA
Sungaiguntung
INDONESIA

© RMcN.   Scale 1:3,000,000; one inch to 47 miles.

ICELAND

ATLANTIC
OCEAN

Reykjavík • Akureyri

Arctic Circle

NORWEGIAN
SEA

NORWAY   SWEDEN

FAEROE IS.
(Den.)

Trondheim

Bergen
Oslo

Stavanger

Stockholm

SHETLAND
ISLANDS
Lerwick

ORKNEY
ISLANDS

SCOTLAND

Glasgow Dundee UNITED
Aberdeen

DENMARK

Göteborg

Copenhagen
(København)

Malmö

BALTIC SEA

IRELAND

Galway Dublin
Limerick
Cork

Belfast
Liverpool

Manchester
BIRMINGHAM
WALES
Cardiff

NORTHERN IRELAND

Edinburgh
Newcastle
upon Tyne

KINGDOM

Kingston upon Hull

Leicester
ENGLAND

NETHERLANDS
Amsterdam

The Hague
('s-Gravenhage)
Rotterdam

NORTH
SEA

HAMBURG

Bremen

BERLIN

POLAND

Hannover Magdeburg

GERMANY

Szczecin

Gdańsk

Poznań

Łódź

WARS
(WARS

Southampton
LONDON
Portsmouth

Plymouth

Cherbourg

BELGIUM
Brussels

Lille

Essen
Bonn

Frankfurt

Leipzig
Dresden

CZECH
REPUBLIC

PRAGUE
(PRAHA)

Wrocław

Ostrava

Katowice

Kraké

Brest
Rennes

Le Havre
Rouen

LUX.
Luxembourg

Mainz

Nürnberg

Stuttgart

MUNICH
(MÜNCHEN)

VIENNA
(WIEN)

SLOVAKIA

Bratislava

PARIS

Nantes

Orléans

Tours

FRANCE

Strasbourg

Zürich

Dijon

SWITZERLAND
Bern

AUSTRIA

BUDAPEST

HUNGARY

Győr Debrecen

Graz

Limoges

Lausanne

Lyon

MILAN
(MILANO)

SLOVENIA

Ljubljana

Zagreb

CROATIA

Szeged

Timiş

La Coruña
Vigo

Gijón Santander
Oviedo

Bilbao

Bordeaux

Toulouse

PYRENEES

ANDORRA

Turin
(Torino)

Genoa
(Genova)

Venice
(Venezia)

SAN
MARINO

Bologna

BELGRADE
(BEOGRAD)

BOSNIA AND
HERZEGOVINA

Sarajevo

Porto

Salamanca

Valladolid

Zaragoza

Marseille

Nice

MONACO

La Spezia
Livorno

Florence
(Firenze)

Ancona

Split

YUGOSLAV

PORTUGAL

Lisbon
(Lisboa)

Badajoz

MADRID

Toledo

SPAIN

Barcelona

Tarragona

Toulon

CORSICA
(Fr.)

Ajaccio

ITALY

ROME
(ROMA)

ALBANIA

Bari

Tiranë

Córdoba

Sevilla

Granada

Albacete

Murcia

València

Alacant

BALEARIC ISLANDS

Palma

MALLORCA

MENORCA

EIVISSA

SARDINIA
(It.)

NAPLES
(NAPOLI)

Taranto

Lecce

Cádiz

Málaga

GIBRALTAR (U.K.)

Tanger

Almería

Cartagena

Cagliari

Palermo

TYRRHENIAN
SEA

Cosenza

Messina

Catanzaro

Rabat

MOROCCO

Melilla
(Sp.)

ALGIERS
(EL DJAZAÏR)

Wahran

Annaba

Tunis

SICILY
(It.)

Catania

IONIAN
SEA

Casablanca

Fès

Meknès

ALGERIA

Qacentina

Batna

TUNISIA

Sousse

MALTA

MEDITERRANEAN

Marrakech

Scale 1:16,000,000; one inch to 252 miles
Lambert Conformal Conic Projection

Scale 1:10,000,000; one inch to 158 miles
Lambert Conformal Conic Projection

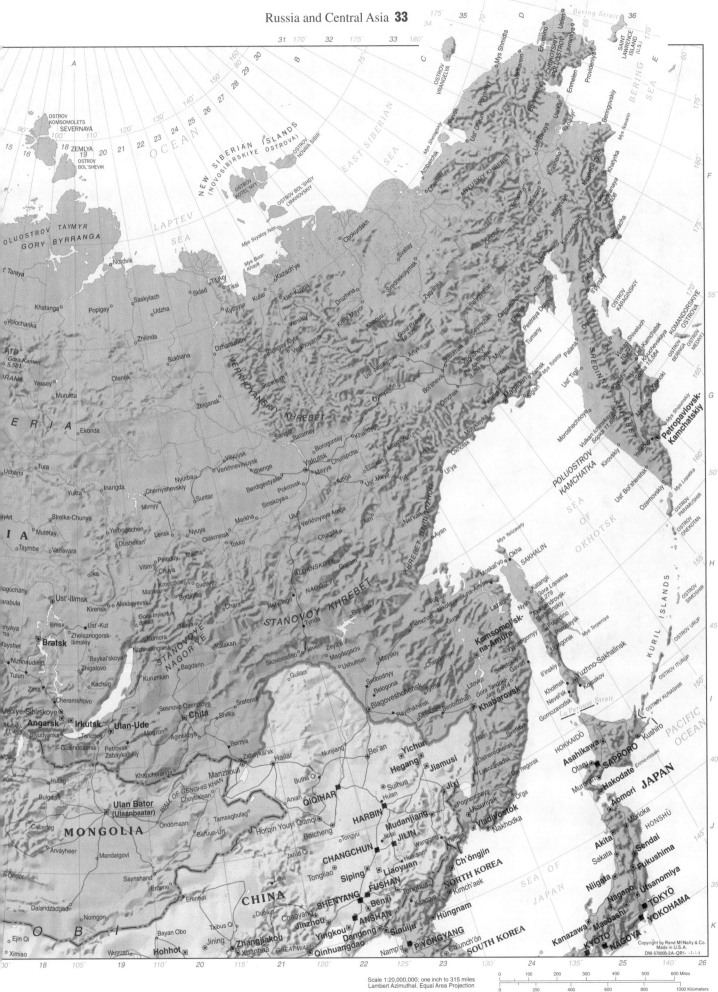

Scale 1:20,000,000; one inch to 315 miles
Lambert Azimuthal, Equal Area Projection

| 0 | 100 | 200 | 300 | 400 | 500 | 600 Miles |

| 0 | 200 | 400 | 600 | 800 | 1000 Kilometers |

Scale 1:16,000,000; one inch to 252 miles
Lambert Conformal Conic Projection

Tropic of Cancer

OKINO-TORI-SHIMA
(Japan)

MAUG ISLANDS

PHILIPPINE

SEA

NORTHERN MARIANA

MARIANA

ISLANDS

ISLANDS

SARAGON

(U.S.)

SAIPAN

PHILIPPINES

P A C I F I C   O C E A N

GUAM
(U.S.)   Agana

aga

Legaspi

SAMAR

LEYTE

Tacloban

acolod

Cebu

Tagbilaran

umaguete

Sibuyan Sea

Butuan

SOROL

YAP

Cagayan de Oro

Marawi

jian

Bislig

GAFEKUT

FEDERATED STATES OF

MICRONESIA

MINDANAO

abato

*Mount
Apo
9,692*

Davao

Koronadal

Cape San Agustin

PALAU ISLANDS

Koror

General Santos

*Tinaca
Point*

SONSORAL
ISLANDS

PALAU (BELAU)

KEPULAUAN
TALAUD

C A R O L I N E   I S L A N D S

Tahuna

MOROTAI

Wayabula

Galela

Manado

Gunung Klabat 6,634

HALMAHERA

Equator

Tondano

Weda

*Molucca Sea
(Laut Maluku)*

uk

labuha

Sorong

Manokwari

MANUS
ISLAND

Patusi

Laiwui

Jazirah Doberai

Bosnik

Teba

Tanjung D'Urville

Kavieng

KEPULAUAN OBI

PULAU MISOOL

Serui

Sarmi

KEPULAUAN SULU

*Ceram Sea
(Laut Seram)*

Kokas

Waren

Jayapura

B I S M A R C K   A R C H I P E L A G O

Namlea

Piru

CERAM (SERAM)

Bula

*Semenanjung
Bomberai*

Wewak

Bogia

BURU

E   **S**   **I**   **A**

Ambon

P E G U N U N G A N   M A O K E

NEW   GUINEA

Madang

*Puncak
Jaya
16,503*

*Puncak
Trikora
15,584*

CENTRAL RANGE

Mount Hagen

Mount
Wilhelm
14,793

Aisega

Tual

Dobo

*Puncak
Mandala
15,617*

Hoskins

*Banda Sea
(Laut Banda)*

(M A L U K U)

Birab

Lake
Murray

Mount
Giluwe
14,330

Goroka

Lae

Cape Cretin

NEW BRITAIN

KEPULAUAN BARAT DAYA

PULAU YAMDENA

Kepi

**PAPUA NEW
GUINEA**

KEPULAUAN
ARU

Tanjung De Jongs

Digul

Kerema

Tepa

Dili

Saumlaki

PULAU YOS
SUDARSO

Losuia

Tutuala

ARAFURA SEA

Tanjung Vals

Merauke

*Gulf of
Papua*

Popondetta

Tufi

Ocussi

TIMOR

Mari

Daru

OWEN STANLEY RANGE

Esa'ala

Soe

Timor Sea

Port Moresby

Samarai

Torres Strait

Bamaga   *Cape York*

Scale 1:16,000,000; one inch to 252 miles
Sinusoidal Projection

| 0 | 100 | 200 | 300 | 400 | 500 Miles |

| 0 | 200 | 400 | 600 | 800 Kilometers |

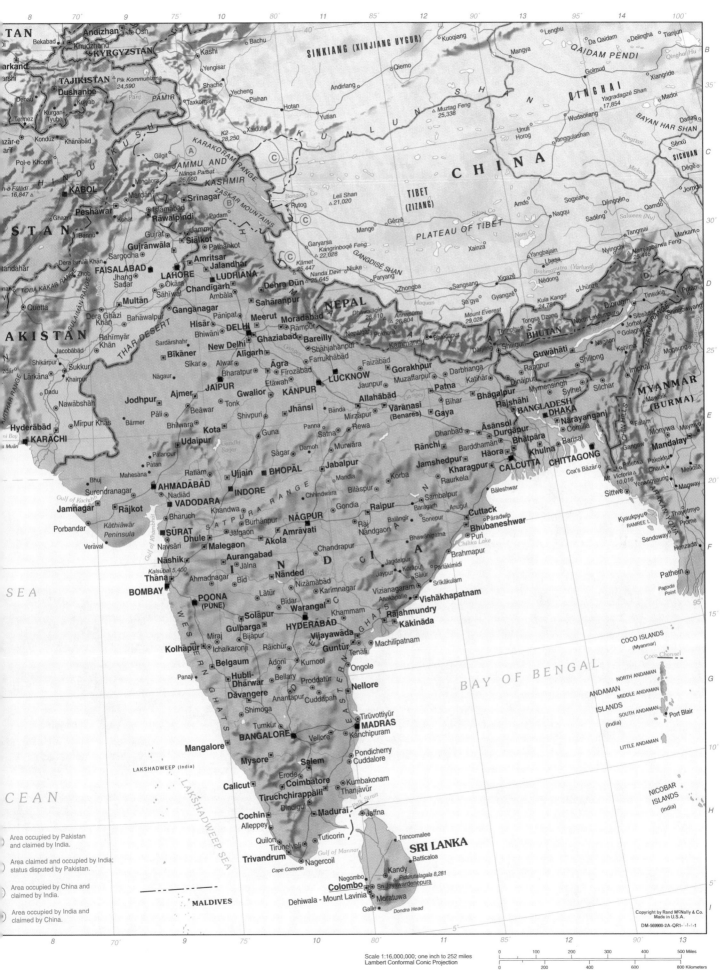

Scale 1:16,000,000; one inch to 252 miles
Lambert Conformal Conic Projection

| 0 | 100 | 200 | 300 | 400 | 500 Miles |

| 0 | 200 | 400 | 600 | 800 Kilometers |

Area occupied by Pakistan and claimed by India.

Area claimed and occupied by India; status disputed by Pakistan.

Area occupied by China and claimed by India.

Area occupied by India and claimed by China.

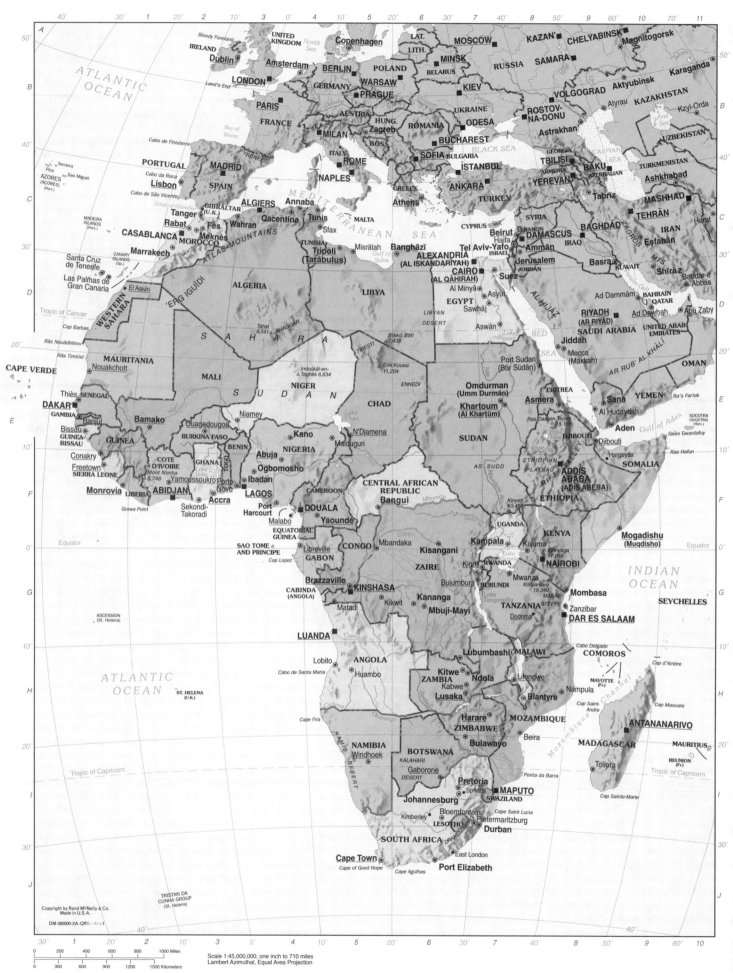

Scale 1:45,000,000; one inch to 710 miles
Lambert Azimuthal, Equal Area Projection

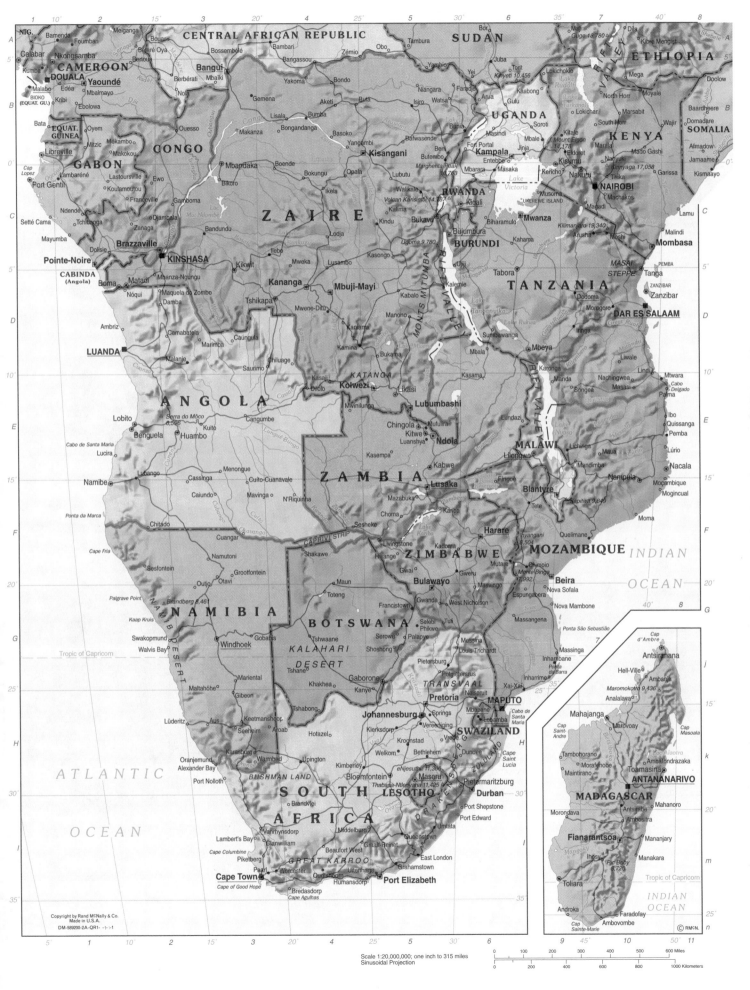

NTG.

A
Bamenda
Fournban
Meiganga
Bouar
CENTRAL AFRICAN REPUBLIC
Bambari
Obo
Tambura
SUDAN
Bor
Mali 13,780
Dila
Kibre Mengist
Shebele
A
ETHIOPIA

Calabar
Nkongsamba
Betare Oya
Bossembélé
Zémio
Yei
Juba
Torit
Khyeti 10,456
Lokichokio
Mega
Doolow

B
CAMEROON
DOUALA
Bertoua
Berbérati
Mbaïki
Bangui
Yakoma
Bondo
Niangara
Faradje
Kaabong
North Horr
Moyale
Baardheere
Marsabit

Malabo
Edéa
Yaoundé
Nola
Gemena
Buta
Isiro
Watsa
Bunia
Gulu
UGANDA
Mount Elgon 14,178
Eldoret
Marala
Mado Gashi
Wajir
Domadare
Almado

BIOKO (EQUAT. GU.)
Kribi
Mbalmayo
Lisala
Bumba
Bafwasende
Beni
Butembo
Margherita Peak 16,763
Fort Portal
Kampala
Entebbe
Jinja
Kisumu
Kericho
Nakuru
Kinyaga 17,058
Thika
Garissa
Jamaame
Kismaayo

C
EQUAT. GUINEA
Libreville
Oyem
Mékambo
Makokou
Mbandaka
Boende
Bokungu
Opala
Walikale
Volcan Karisimbi 14,787
RWANDA
Kigali
Bukavu
Lake Victoria
UKEREWE ISLAND
Musoma
Machakos
NAIROBI
Lamu

GABON
Cap Lopez
Lambaréné
Lastoursville
Ewo
Ikela
Kindu
Biharamulo
Mwanza
Kilimanjaro 19,340
Arusha
Moshi
Malindi

Port Gentil
Koulamoutou
Franceville
ZAIRE
Lodja
Kalima
Ugoma 9,780
Bujumbura
BURUNDI
Kahama
MASAI STEPPE
Tanga
Mombasa

Setté Cama
Ndendé
Tchibanga
Zanaga
Djambala
Mai Ndombe
Ilebo
Mweka
Lusambo
Kasongo
Kalemie
Tabora
Dodoma
PEMBA
Zanzibar

CONGO
Brazzaville
KINSHASA
Kikwit
Kananga
Mbuji-Mayi
Kabalo
Mtwara

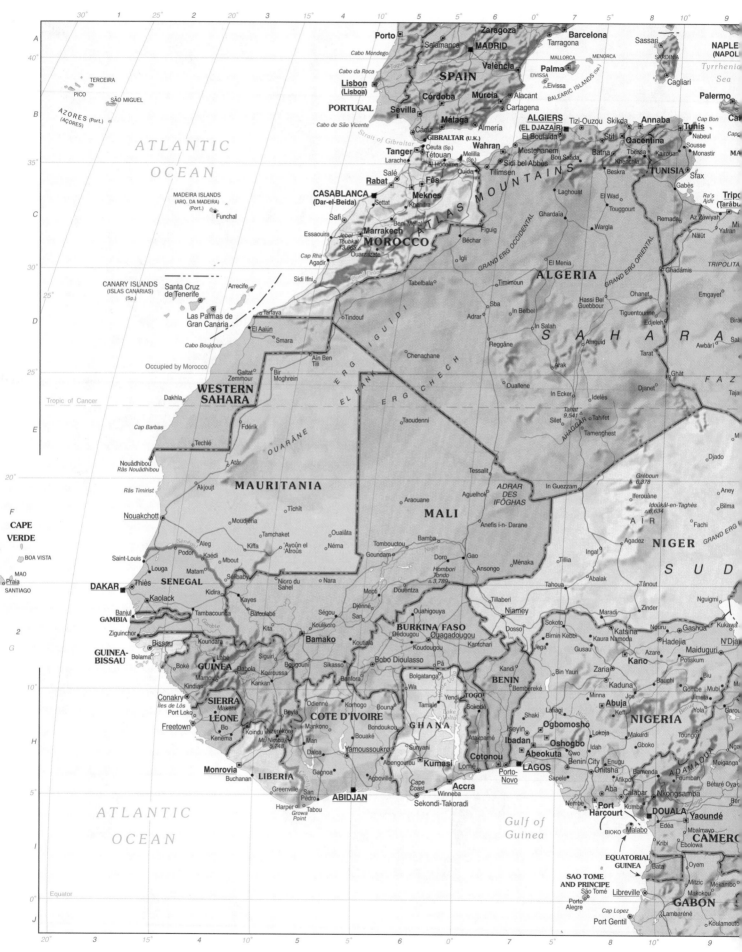

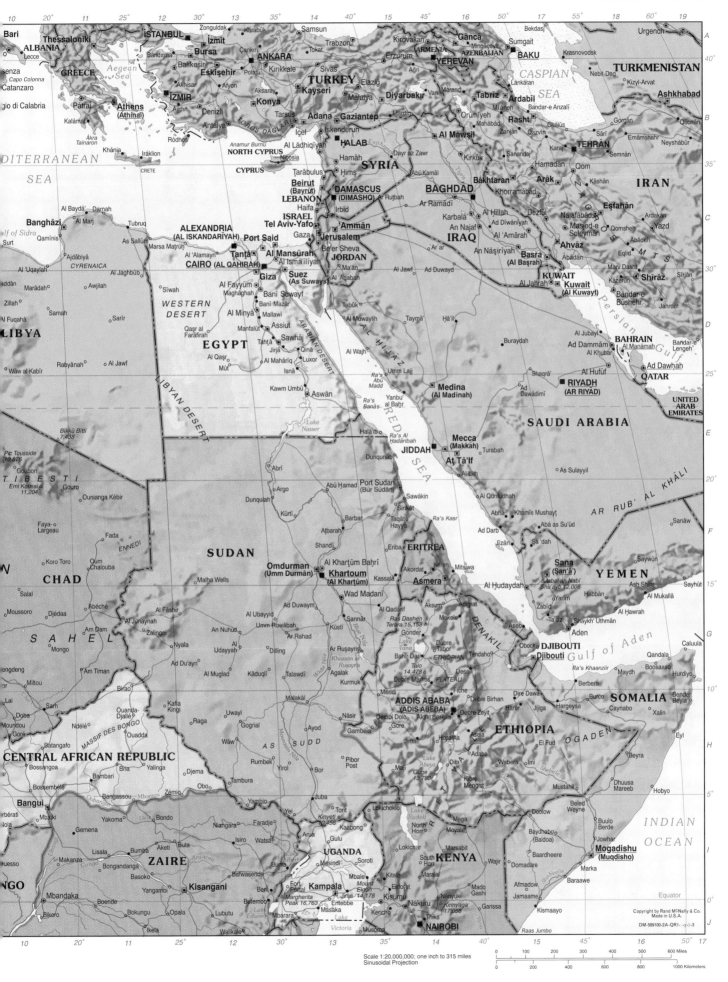

Scale 1:20,000,000; one inch to 315 miles
Sinusoidal Projection

0   100   200   300   400   500   600 Miles

0   200   400   600   800   1000 Kilometers

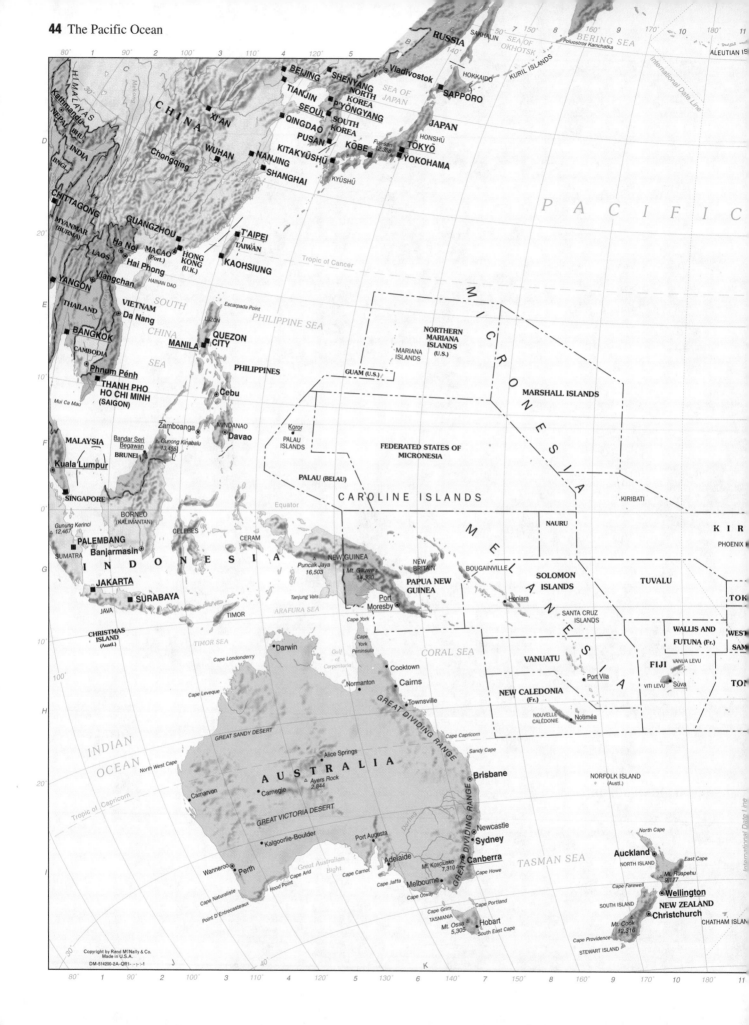

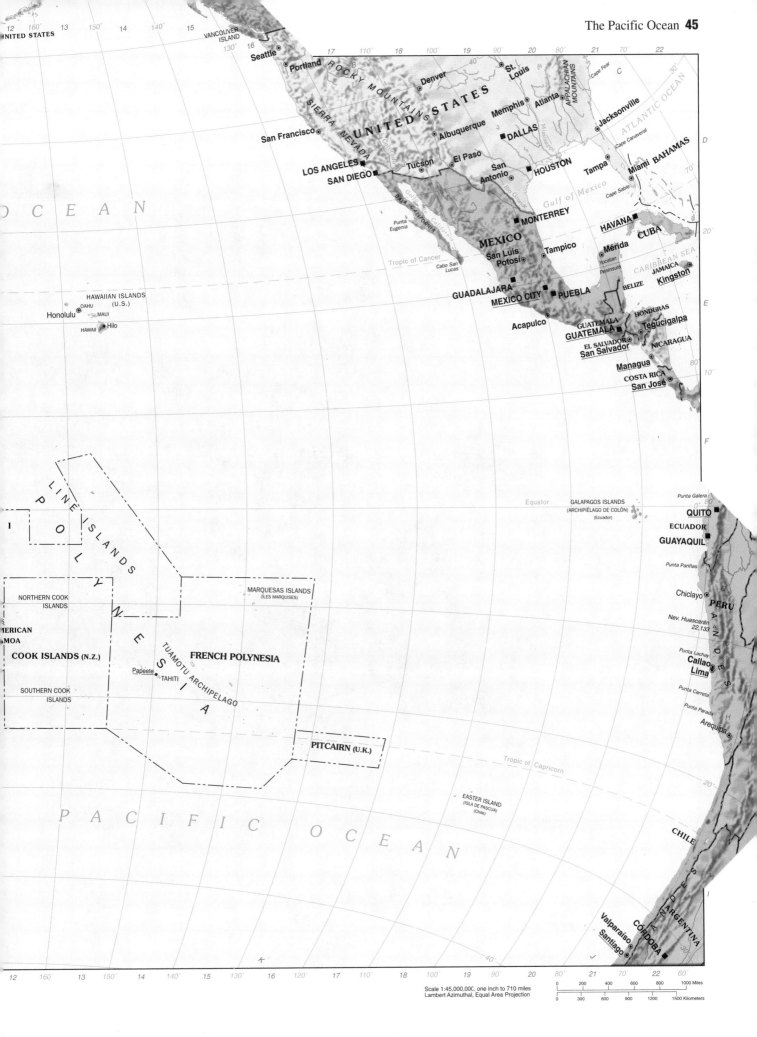

UNITED STATES

Vancouver Island

Seattle
Portland
ROCKY MOUNTAINS
Denver
St. Louis
Cape Fear

SIERRA NEVADA
UNITED STATES
Albuquerque
Memphis
Atlanta
APPALACHIAN MOUNTAINS
Jacksonville

San Francisco
DALLAS
Cape Canaveral

ATLANTIC OCEAN

Tucson
El Paso
San Antonio
HOUSTON
Tampa
Miami BAHAMAS

LOS ANGELES
SAN DIEGO
Cape Sable

Gulf of Mexico

OCEAN

Punta Eugenia
MONTERREY
HAVANA
CUBA

MEXICO
San Luis Potosí
Tampico
Mérida
CARIBBEAN SEA
JAMAICA
Kingston

Tropic of Cancer
Cabo San Lucas
Yucatán
Yucatan Peninsula
BELIZE

HAWAIIAN ISLANDS (U.S.)
GUADALAJARA
MEXICO CITY
PUEBLA
HONDURAS

Honolulu
OAHU
MAUI
Acapulco
GUATEMALA
GUATEMALA
Tegucigalpa

HAWAII
Hilo
EL SALVADOR
San Salvador
NICARAGUA

Managua
Manague

COSTA RICA
San José

Punta Galera
GALAPAGOS ISLANDS (ARCHIPIÉLAGO DE COLÓN) (Ecuador)
Equator
QUITO

ECUADOR
GUAYAQUIL

LINE ISLANDS
POLYNESIA
Punta Pariñas

I
Chiclayo
PERU

NORTHERN COOK ISLANDS
MARQUESAS ISLANDS (ÎLES MARQUISES)
Nev. Huascarán 22,133

AMERICAN SAMOA
Punta Lachay
Callao
Lima

COOK ISLANDS (N.Z.)
TUAMOTU ARCHIPELAGO
FRENCH POLYNESIA

Papeete
TAHITI
Punta Carreta

SOUTHERN COOK ISLANDS
Punta Parada
Arequipa

PITCAIRN (U.K.)
Tropic of Capricorn

EASTER ISLAND (ISLA DE PASCUA) (Chile)

PACIFIC   OCEAN

CHILE

ARGENTINA

Valparaíso
Santiago
CÓRDOBA

Scale 1:45,000,000; one inch to 710 miles
Lambert Azimuthal, Equal Area Projection

200   400   600   800   1000 Miles
0   300   600   900   1200   1500 Kilometers

INDONESIA

BORNEO
Palangkaraya
Banjarmasin
Martapura
Tanjung Selatan

Parepare
Watampone
Singkang
CELEBES
Sindjai
Baubau
Ujungpandang
Bantaeng

SEMARANG
Sumenep
Surakarta
Surabaya
Banyuwangi
Madium
Kedin
Malang
Denpasar
JAVA
(JAWA)

SUMBAWA
Mataram
Raba
Reo
FLORES
Ende
Soe
Waingapu
Kupang
SUMBA
TIMOR
Dili
Ocussi

Tual
KEPULAUAN
ARU
Birab

NEW GUINEA

PAP
NE
GUI

Meyanodas
PULAU
YAMDENA

Tanjung Vals
Merauke
Da

ARAFURA SEA

Torres Strait
Bamaga
Cape Yo
Cape York
Weipa
Peninsula

Cape Van Diemen
Cape Londonderry

TIMOR SEA

Cape
Croker
Coburg Pen.
Van Diemen
Gulf
Darwin
ARNHEM LAND
Pine
Creek
Cape Arnhem
GROOTE
EYLANDT
Cape Beatrice

Cape
Wessel
Duifken Point
York

Gulf of
Carpentaria

INDIAN
OCEAN

Joseph
Bonaparte Gulf

KIMBERLEY
PLATEAU
Mt. Hann
2,556
Wyndham
Mt. Ord
3,074
DURACK RANGES
KING LEOPOLD RANGES

Daly
Mataranka

NORTHERN
Hooker Creek
Newcastle
Waters
Burketown
Normanton

Cape Leveque
Yeeda
Broome
Fitzroy
Christmas
Creek
Halls
Creek

Victoria
BARKLY TABLELAND
Camooweal
Cloncurry
Hughen
GREGORY RANGE

Cape Latouche Treville
EIGHTY MILE BEACH

TANAMI
DESERT
The Granites
Tennant
Creek
Mount Isa

TERRITORY
Winton

GREAT ARTESIAN
BASIN
Longre

Port Hedland
Marble Bar
Nullagine
GREAT SANDY DESERT
Lake
Auld

Mt. Leisler
2,943
Mt. Liebig
5,000
Mt. Zeil
4,957
Alice
Springs
MacDonnell Ranges

Dampier
Yarraloola
HAMERSLEY RANGE
Mt. Brockman
3,714
Mt. Bruce
4,052
Ethel
Creek

AUSTRALIA
SIMPSON
DESERT

Yar

QUE

North West Cape
Onslow
Mt. Meharry
4,104

WESTERN
GIBSON DESERT
Mt. Cockburn
3,734
Ayers Rock
2,844

Cape Cuvier
Mt. Augustus
3,625
Lake
Carnegie
Carnegie
Mt. Aloysius
3,560
Mt. Woodroffe
4,724

Lake
Eyre
North
STURT
STONY
DESERT

Innamincka
Thargominda
GRE
Milparinka

Minilya
Carnarvon
Wooramet
Shark Bay
DIRK HARTOG
ISLAND

AUSTRALIA
Wiluna
Meekatharra
Sandstone
White
Cliffs
Leonora

SOUTH AUSTRALIA
Marree

Tropic of Capricorn

Bluff Point
Mount
Magnet
Leonora
GREAT VICTORIA DESERT
Mount Eba
Kingoonya
Saint Mary
Peak 3,871
Lake
Torrens
BARRIER
RANGE
Wilc

Geraldton
Mullewa
Paynes Find
NULLARBOR PLAIN
Ceduna
Eucla
Lake
Gairdner

Broken Hill
NEW

Dongara
Coolgardie
Kalgoorlie-Boulder
Streaky Bay
Port Augusta
Whyalla
Eyre
Peninsula
Port Pirie
Mildura

DARLING RANGE
Wanneroo
Perth
Gosnells
Armadale
Fremantle
Norseman
Balladonia
Great Australian Bight
Port Lincoln
Cape Carnot
Port
Elizabeth
Adelaide

Geographe Bay
Newdegate
Spencer Gulf
Gulf St Vincent
Murray

Bunbury
Wagin
Hopetoun
KANGAROO
ISLAND
Encounter
Bay
Horsham
Be
Balla

Cape
Naturaliste
Augusta
Bluff Knoll
3,596
Hood
Point
Cape Arid
ARCHIPELAGO OF
THE RECHERCHE
Cape Jaffa
Hamilton
Ge

Cranbrook
Albany
Mount
Gambier
Portland
Cape Otwa

Point D'Entrecasteaux
West
Cape Hope

KING ISLA

INDIAN OCEAN

Cap

TAS

New Britain
Lae
Cape Cretin
Popondetta
SOLOMON SEA
Port Moresby
OWEN STANLEY RANGE
Kulumadau
Samarai

NEW BRITAIN
BOUGAINVILLE
CHOISEUL
SANTA ISABEL

SOLOMON ISLANDS

Honiara
GUADALCANAL
MALAITA

SAN CRISTOBAL

SANTA CRUZ ISLANDS

TUVALU

CORAL SEA

BARRIER REEF

Cairns
Mt le Frere
22
Halifax Bay
Townsville

Mackay
Mt. Dalrymple
4,131
Blair Athol
Rockhampton
Cape Capricorn
Emerald
Gladstone
Springsure
Theodore
Bundaberg
Sandy Cape
Maryborough
FRASER ISLAND
Mitchell
Gympie
Mt. Kiangarow
3,760
Chinchilla
Redcliffe
Toowoomba
Brisbane
Ipswich
Southport
Warwick
Cape Byron
Lismore
Grafton
Coffs Harbour
Armidale
Tamworth
Taree
Nyngan
Dubbo
Taree
WALES
Cessnock
Newcastle
Penrith
Parramatta
Sydney
Goulburn
Campbelltown
Wollongong
A.C.T.
Canberra
Jervis Bay
Cooma
Mt. Kosciusko
2,310
Cape Howe

VANUATU
ÎLES BANKS
ESPIRITU SANTO
PENTECOTE
MALAKULA
EPI
Port Vila
ÉFATÉ
NEW
ERROMANGO
HEBRIDES

NEW CALEDONIA
(Fr.)
NOUVELLE CALÉDONIE
LOYALTY ISLANDS
Nouméa

WALLIS AND FUTUNA (Fr.)

FIJI
VANUA LEVU
Lautoka
VITI LEVU
Suva
KANDUVU ISLAND

PACIFIC
OCEAN

NORFOLK ISLAND
(Austl.)

Tropic of Capricorn

TASMAN SEA

Devonport
Launceston
Freycinet Peninsula
TASMANIA
South East Cape

Sale
Wilsons Promontory
FLINDERS ISLAND
Cape Portland

Cape Maria van Diemen
North Cape
Cape Brett
Whangarei
Needles Point
East Coast Bays
Mount Roskill
Auckland
Manukau
Bay of Plenty
Hamilton
Tauranga
Albatross Point
NORTH ISLAND
New Plymouth
Cape Egmont
Taupo
Mt. Ruapehu
9,177
Rotorua
East Cape
Gisborne
Wanganui
Napier
Cape Farewell
Palmerston North
Hastings
The Twins
5,990
Nelson
Porirua
Greymouth
Waiau
Wellington
Haast
NEW ZEALAND
Jackson Head
SOUTHERN ALPS
Mt. Cook
3,764
SOUTH ISLAND
Ashburton
Christchurch
Timaru
West Cape
Manapouri
Oamaru
Invercargill
Dunedin
STEWART ISLAND

CHATHAM ISLANDS
(N.Z.)

International Date Line

Scale 1:20,000,000; one inch to 315 miles
Lambert's Azimuthal; Equal Area Projection

0 100 200 300 400 500 600 Miles
0 200 400 600 800 1000 Kilometers

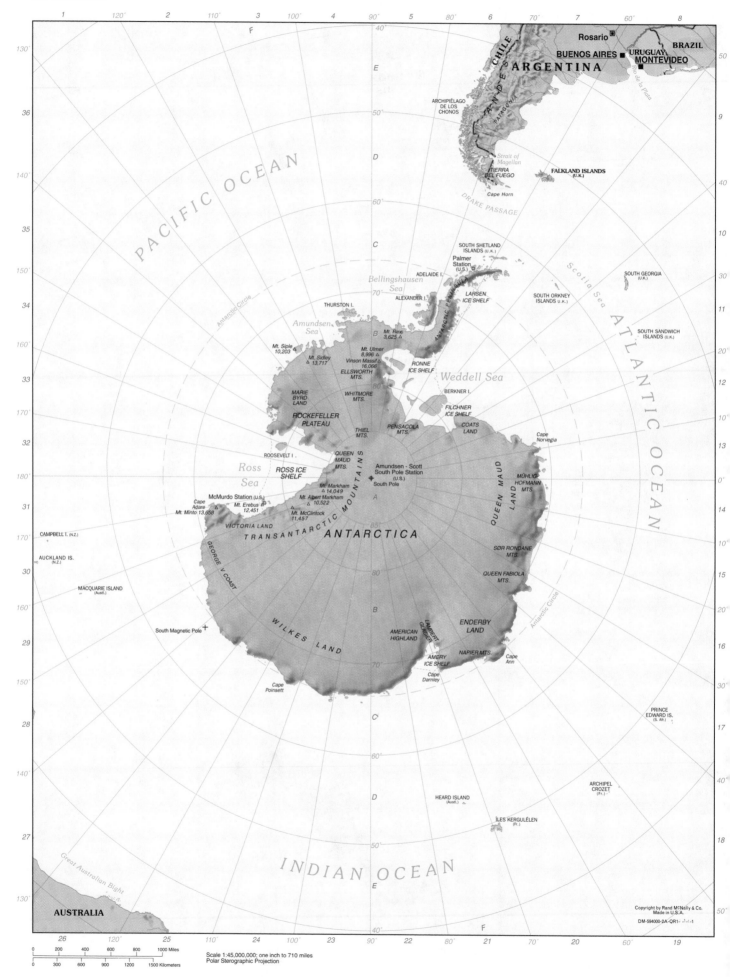

PACIFIC OCEAN

ATLANTIC OCEAN

INDIAN OCEAN

Rosario

BUENOS AIRES

URUGUAY
MONTEVIDEO

BRAZIL

ARGENTINA

CHILE

ANDES

PATAGONIA

ARCHIPIÉLAGO
DE LOS
CHONOS

Strait of
Magellan

TIERRA
DEL FUEGO

Cape Horn

FALKLAND ISLANDS
(U.K.)

Río de la Plata

DRAKE PASSAGE

Scotia Sea

SOUTH GEORGIA
(U.K.)

SOUTH SANDWICH
ISLANDS (U.K.)

SOUTH SHETLAND
ISLANDS (U.K.)

Palmer
Station
(U.S.)

ADELAIDE I.

ALEXANDER I.

LARSEN
ICE SHELF

SOUTH ORKNEY
ISLANDS U.K.

Bellingshausen
Sea

ANTARCTIC CIRCLE

Antarctic Circle

THURSTON I.

Amundsen
Sea

Mt. Siple
10,203

Mt. Sidley
13,717

Mt. Rex
3,625

Mt. Ulmer
8,996

Vinson Massif
16,066

ELLSWORTH
MTS.

RONNE
ICE SHELF

Weddell Sea

BERKNER I.

FILCHNER
ICE SHELF

Cape
Norvegia

MARIE
BYRD
LAND

WHITMORE
MTS.

PENSACOLA
MTS.

COATS
LAND

ROCKEFELLER
PLATEAU

THIEL
MTS.

ROOSEVELT I.

Ross
Sea

ROSS ICE
SHELF

QUEEN
MAUD
MTS.

Amundsen - Scott
South Pole Station
(U.S.)
South Pole

ANTARCTICA

QUEEN MAUD LAND

MÜHLIG-
HOFMANN
MTS.

McMurdo Station (U.S.)

Cape
Adare

Mt. Minto 13,658

Mt. Erebus
12,451

Mt. Markham
14,049

Mt. Albert Markham
10,522

Mt. McClintock
11,457

SØR RONDANE
MTS.

VICTORIA LAND

TRANSANTARCTIC MOUNTAINS

QUEEN FABIOLA
MTS.

CAMPBELL I. (N.Z.)

AUCKLAND IS.
(N.Z.)

GEORGE V COAST

South Magnetic Pole

WILKES LAND

AMERICAN
HIGHLAND

LAMBERT GLACIER

ENDERBY
LAND

NAPIER MTS.

Cape
Ann

Antarctic Circle

MACQUARIE ISLAND
(Aust.)

AMERY
ICE SHELF

Cape
Darnley

Cape
Poinsett

PRINCE
EDWARD IS.
(S. Afr.)

Great Australian Bight

ARCHIPEL
CROZET
(Fr.)

HEARD ISLAND
(Austl.)

ÎLES KERGUÉLEN
(Fr.)

AUSTRALIA

0 200 400 600 800 1000 Miles

0 300 600 900 1200 1500 Kilometers

Scale 1:45,000,000; one inch to 710 miles
Polar Sterographic Projection

Index

The names of cities appear in the index in regular type. The names of all other features appear in *italics,* followed by descriptive terms (*cont., mtn., terr.*) to indicate their nature.

Abbreviations of Geographical names and terms

Ak., U.S.	Alaska
Al., U.S.	Alabama
Ant.	Antarctica
Ar., U.S.	Arkansas
Arg.	Argentina
Asia	Asia
Austl.	Australia
Az., U.S.	Arizona
b.	bay, gulf
Bah.	Bahrain
B.C., Can.	British Columbia
Bol.	Bolivia
Braz.	Brazil
c.	cape, point
Ca., U.S.	California
Can.	Canada
Cay. Is.	Cayman Islands
Co., U.S.	Colorado
Col.	Colombia
cont.	continent
C.R.	Costa Rica
ctry.	country
D.C., U.S.	District of Columbia
De., U.S.	Delaware
dep.	dependency
Dom. Rep.	Dominican Republic
El Sal.	El Salvador
Eng., U.K.	England
Fl., U.S.	Florida
Ga., U.S.	Georgia
Guad.	Guadeloupe
hist. reg.	historic region
H.K.	Hong Kong
Hond.	Honduras
i.	island
Ia., U.S.	Iowa
Id., U.S.	Idaho
Il., U.S.	Illinois
In., U.S.	Indiana
Ire.	Ireland
is.	islands
Jam.	Jamaica
Ks., U.S.	Kansas
Ky., U.S.	Kentucky
l.	lake
La., U.S.	Louisiana
Leb.	Lebanon
Ma., U.S.	Massachusetts
Malay.	Malaysia
Md., U.S.	Maryland
Me., U.S.	Maine
Mex.	Mexico
Mi., U.S.	Michigan
Mn., U.S.	Minnesota
Mo., U.S.	Missouri
Monts.	Montserrat
Mor.	Morocco
Ms., U.S.	Mississippi
Mt., U.S.	Montana
mtn.	mountain
mts.	mountains
N.A.	North America
Nb., U.S.	Nebraska
N.C., U.S.	North Carolina
N.D., U.S.	North Dakota
Newf., Can.	Newfoundland
N.H., U.S.	New Hampshire
Nic.	Nicaragua
N.M., U.S.	New Mexico
N.S., Can.	Nova Scotia
Nv., U.S.	Nevada
N.W.T., Can.	Northwest Territories
N.Y., U.S.	New York
N.Z.	New Zealand
Oh., U.S.	Ohio
Ok., U.S.	Oklahoma
Ont., Can.	Ontario
Or., U.S.	Oregon
Pa., U.S.	Pennsylvania
Pak.	Pakistan
Pan.	Panama
Para.	Paraguay
pen.	peninsula
Phil.	Philippines
plat.	plateau
pol. div.	political division
P.R.	Puerto Rico
prov.	province
res.	reservoir
Sask., Can.	Saskatchewan
S.C., U.S.	South Carolina
Scot., U.K.	Scotland
S.D., U.S.	South Dakota
Sen.	Senegal
Sri L.	Sri Lanka
St. K./N.	St. Kitts and Nevis
stm.	river, stream
strt.	strait
terr.	territory
Tn., U.S.	Tennessee
Trin.	Trinidad and Tobago
Tx., U.S.	Texas
U.K.	United Kingdom
Urug.	Uruguay
U.S.	United States
Ut., U.S.	Utah
Va., U.S.	Virginia
Ven.	Venezuela
vol.	volcano
Vt., U.S.	Vermont
Wa., U.S.	Washington
Wi., U.S.	Wisconsin
W.V., U.S.	West Virginia
Wy., U.S.	Wyoming

A

Aba H-8 42
Ābādān C-4 38
Abaetetuba D-9 23
Abakan G-16 32
Abancay F-4 22
Abay H-12 32
Abeokuta H-7 42
Aberdeen, Scot., U.K. D-5 28
Aberdeen, S.C., U.S. D-7 12
Abidjan H-6 42
Abilene J-7 13
Abu Dhaby, see Abū Ẓaby E-5 38
Abuja H-8 42
Abū Ẓaby (Abu Dhabi) E-5 38
Acámbaro G-9 19
Acapulco I-10 19
Acarigua B-5 22
Accra H-6 42
Achinsk F-16 32
Aconcagua, Cerro, mtn. C-3 21
Acre, state E-4 22
Actopan G-10 19
Ada J-8 13
Adamaoua, mts. H-9 42
Adana H-13 27
Adare, Cape B-31 48
Ad Dammām D-4 38
Ad Dawḩah D-5 38
Addis Ababa (Adis Abeba) H-14 43
Adelaide H-6 46
Aden ('Adan) G-4 38
Aden, Gulf of G-4 38
Adirondack Mountains D-9 10
Adrar D-6 42
Adriatic Sea D-7 31
Aegean Sea E-8 31
Afghanistan, ctry. C-7 38
Africa, cont. F-14 3
'Afula m-24 25
Agadir C-5 42
Agana C-11 37
Āgra D-10 39
Ağrı Dağı, mtn H-14 27
Agua Prieta B-5 18
Aguascalientes G-8 18
Aguascalientes, state F-8 18
Ahaggar, mts. E-8 42
Ahmadābād E-9 39
Ahvāz C-4 38
Aiken J-6 11
Ajaccio D-5 30
Ajmer D-9 39
Akita D-16 35
'Akko m-24 25
Aklavik C-6 6
Akmola (Tselinograd) G-12 32
Akola E-10 39
Akordat F-14 43
Akron F-6 10
Aktau I-8 33
Aktyubinsk G-12 32
Al Khubar D-5 38
Alabama, stm. K-3 11
Alabama, state J-3 11
Alacant E-3 30
Alagoas, state E-11 23
Alagoinhas F-11 23
Alajuela F-8 17
Al 'Alamayn C-12 43
Alamogordo L-12 15
Alamosa H-4 13
Åland (Ahvenanmaa), i. C-9 29
Al 'Aqabah p-24 25
Al 'Arīsh n-22 25
Alaska, state B-6 5
Alaska, Gulf of D-7 5
Alaska Peninsula D-5 5
Alaska Range, mts. C-6 5
Albacete E-3 30
Albania, ctry. D-7 31
Albany, Austl. G-2 46
Albany, Ga., U.S. K-4 11
Albany, N.Y., U.S. E-10 10
Albany, Or., U.S. F-3 14
Al Bayda' C-11 43
Albert, Lake B-6 41
Alberta, prov. E-10 6
Albert Lea E-10 12
Ålborg D-8 28
Albuquerque K-11 15
Albury H-8 47
Alcalá de Henares D-3 30
Alchev'sk C-11 31
Aldan, stm. F-24 33
Aldanskoye Nagor'ye, plat. F-23 33
Aleksandrovsk-Sakhalinskiy G-26 33
Ålesund C-7 28
Aleutian Islands f-14 5
Alexandria (Al Iskandarīyah), Egypt C-12 43
Alexandria, La., U.S. K-10 13
Alexandria, Va., U.S. G-8 10
Aleysk G-14 32
Al Fāshir G-12 43
Al Fayyūm D-13 43
Algeria, ctry. D-7 42
Algiers (El Djazaïr) B-7 42
Al Hoceïma B-6 42
Al Hufūf D-4 38
Alice Springs E-5 46
Alīgarh D-10 39
Al Ismā'īlīyah C-13 43
Al Ismā'īlīyah o-21 25
Al Jawf D-11 43
Al Junaynah G-11 43
Al Khalīl n-24 25
Al Kharṭūm Baḩrī F-13 43
Al Khums C-9 42
Al Lādhiqīyah B-2 38
Allahābād D-11 39
Allegheny, stm. F-7 10
Allentown F-9 10
Alma-Ata (Almaty) I-13 32
Almalyk I-11 32
Al Manāmah D-5 38
Al Manṣūrah C-13 43
Al Marj C-11 43
Al-Mawṣil B-3 38
Almería E-3 30
Al Minyā D-13 43
Alor Setar D-3 36
Alpena D-5 10
Alps, mts. C-5 30
Al Qaḑārif G-14 43
Alta Floresta F-7 23
Altagracia A-4 22
Altai, mts. H-15 32
Altamira D-8 23
Altamont G-4 14
Altiplano, plain G-5 22
Alton G-11 12
Altun Shan, mts. D-6 34
Alturas H-4 14
Altus I-7 13
Amapá, state C-8 23
Amarillo I-6 13
Amazon (Amazonas), stm. D-8 23
Amazonas, state D-6 22
Ambarchik D-30 33
Ambato D-3 22
Ambon F-8 37
American Highland B-22 48
American Samoa, dep. H-12 45
Americus J-4 11
Amiens C-4 30
'Ammān C-2 38
Amrāvati E-10 39
Amritsar C-10 39
Amsterdam E-7 28
Amu Darya, stm. I-10 32
Amundsen Sea B-2 48
Amur, stm. G-25 33
Anadyr' E-33 33
Anápolis G-9 23
Anchorage C-7 5
Ancona D-6 31
Andaman Islands C-1 36
Andaman Sea C-2 36
Anderson I-5 11
Andes, mts. -0 20
Andizhan I-12 33
Andong D-13 35
Andorra, ctry. D-4 30
Andros, i. D-9 17
Angara, stm. F-18 33
Ángel de la Guarda, Isla, i. C-3 18
Angeles B-7 36
Angers C-3 30
Angola, ctry. E-3 41
Anguilla, ctry. E-12 17
Anhui, prov. E-11 35
Ankara H-12 27
Annaba B-8 42
An Najaf C-3 38
Annapolis G-8 10
Ann Arbor E-5 10
Anniston J-4 11
Anshan C-12 35
Antalya H-12 27
Antananarivo k-10 41
Antarctica, cont. A-26 48
Antigua and Barbuda, ctry. E-12 17
Antofagasta A-2 21
Antsiranana j-10 41
Antwerpen E-6 28
A'nyêmaqên Shan, mts. D-8 34
Anyuskiy Khrebet, mts. D-31 33
Anzhero-Sudzhensk F-15 32
Aomori C-16 35
Aôral, Phnum, mtn. C-3 36
Apatzingán H-8 18
Apia H-11 44
Apo, Mount D-8 37
Appalachian Mountains H-6 11
Appennino Mountains D-6 30
Appleton D-12 12
Apure, stm. B-5 22
Aqaba, Gulf of D-1 38
Arabian Desert D-13 43
Arabian Sea F-7 38
Aracaju F-11 23
Araçatuba H-8 23
Arad C-8 31
Arafura Sea B-7 46
Araguaína E-9 23
Arāk C-4 38
Aral Sea H-9 32
Aral'sk H-10 32
Araouane F-6 42
Araraquara H-9 23
Arauca, stm. B-5 22
Arcata H-2 15
Arctic Bay B-16 7
Arctic Ocean A-1 2
Arctic Red, stm. C-7 6
Arctic Village B-7 5
Ardabīl B-4 38
Ardmore I-8 13
Arequipa G-4 22
Argentina, ctry. D-4 21
Argentino, Lago, l. G-2 21
Århus D-8 28
Arica G-4 22
Arīḩā (Jericho) n-24 25
Arizona, state K-9 15
Arkadelphia I-10 13
Arkalyk G-11 32
Arkansas, stm. I-10 13
Arkansas, state I-10 13
Arlington J-8 13
Armadale G-2 46
Armenia C-3 22
Armenia, ctry. G-14 27
Armidale G-9 47
Arnhem, Cape C-6 46
Arnhem Land, region C-5 46
Arrecife D-4 42
Ar Rub' al Khāli, desert F-5 38
Artemisa D-8 17
Artemovsk G-16 32
Artesia L-12 15
Aruba, ctry. F-10 17
Arviat D-15 7
Arzamas F-6 32
Asahikawa C-16 35
Āsānsol E-12 39
Aseb G-15 43
Ashburton I-13 47
Asheville I-5 11
Ashkhabad (Ashgabat) J-9 32
Ashland G-5 10
Ash Shariqah D-6 38
Ashtabula F-6 10
Asia, cont. D-18 3
Asino F-15 32
Asmera F-14 43
Aspen G-3 12
As Sudd, region H-13 43
As Sulaymānīyah B-4 38
Astoria E-3 14
Astrakhan H-7 32
Asunción B-5 21
Aswān E-13 43
Asyūt D-13 43
Atascadero K-4 15
Aṭbarah F-13 43
Atbasar G-11 32
Atchafalaya Bay L-11 13
Atchison G-9 12
Athabasca F-11 6
Athabasca, Lake E-12 6
Athens (Athínai), Greece E-8 31
Athens, Ga., U.S. J-5 11
Athens, Tn., U.S. I-4 11
Atlanta J-4 11
Atlantic City G-9 10
Atlantic Ocean E-10 2
Atlas Mountains C-6 42
At Tā'if E-3 38
Atyrau H-8 32
Auburn, Al., U.S. J-4 11
Auburn, Me., U.S. E-11 10
Auckland H-13 47
Augsburg C-6 30
Augusta, Austl. G-2 46
Augusta, Ga., U.S. J-6 11
Augusta, Me., U.S. D-12 10
Aurangabad F-10 39
Aurora G-4 12
Austin, Mn., U.S. E-10 12
Austin, Tx., U.S. K-8 13
Australia, ctry. E-5 46
Australian Capital Territory, terr. H-8 47
Austria, ctry. C-6 31
Avellaneda C-5 21
Avignon D-4 30
Ayaguz H-14 32
Ayers Rock, mtn. F-6 46
Ayeyarwady, stm. A-1 36
Azerbaijan, ctry. G-15 27
Azores, is. B-1 42
Azov, Sea of C-11 31
Az-Zarqā' C-2 38
Az Zāwiyah C-9 42

B

Bacolod C-7 37
Badajoz D-2 30
Badlands, region D-5 12
Baffin Bay B-20 7
Baffin Island B-17 7
Baghdād C-3 38
Bago B-2 36
Baguio B-7 36
Bahama Islands C-9 17
Bahamas, ctry. C-9 17

D

E

F

Morón D-9 17
Morris G-14 6
Moscow, Id., U.S. E-6 14
Moscow (Moskva), Russia F-5 32
Moses Lake E-5 14
Mosjøen B-8 28
Mosquitos, Golfo de los, b. G-8 17
Mossoró E-11 23
Moultrie K-5 11
Mountain Home G-7 14
Mountain Nile, stm. H-13 43
Mountain View g-20 5
Mount Airy H-6 11
Mount Gambier H-7 46
Mount Isa E-6 46
Mount Magnet F-2 46
Mount Roskill H-13 47
Mount Vernon, Il., U.S. H-12 13
Mount Vernon, Ky., U.S. H-4 11
Mount Vernon, Wa., U.S. D-3 14
Mozambique, ctry. F-6 41
Mozyr' E-11 29
Mudanjiang C-13 35
Mulhouse C-5 30
Multān C-9 39
Munich (München) C-6 30
Münster B-5 30
Murcia E-3 30
Mures, stm. C-8 31
Murmansk D-4 32
Murray H-2 11
Murray, stm. H-7 46
Musala, mtn. D-8 30
Muskegon E-3 10
Muskogee I-9 13
Muztag, mtn. D-5 34
Mwanza C-6 41
Mweru, Lake D-5 41
Myanmar (Burma), ctry. B-2 36
Mykolayiv C-10 31
Mymensingh E-13 39
Myrtle Beach J-7 11
Mysore G-10 39
My Tho C-4 36

N

Naberezhnyye Chelny F-8 32
Nābulus m-24 25
Nacala E-8 41
Naga F-7 37
Nagano D-15 35
Nagasaki E-13 35
Nagoya D-15 35
Nāgpur E-10 39
Naha F-13 35
Nairobi C-7 41
Nakhodka I-24 33
Nakhon Ratchasima C-3 36
Nakhon Si Thammarat D-3 36
Nal'chik I-6 32
Namangan I-12 32
Nam Co, l. E-6 34
Nam Dinh A-4 36
Namib Desert G-2 41
Namibe F-2 41
Namibia, ctry. G-3 41
Namjagbarwa Feng, mtn. F-7 34
Nampa G-6 14
Namp'o D-13 35
Nampula F-7 41
Namur E-6 28
Nanchang F-11 35
Nancy C-5 30
Nānded F-10 39
Nanjing E-11 35
Nanning G-9 34
Nantes C-3 30
Nantong E-12 35
Nantucket Island F-11 10
Nantucket Sound F-11 10
Nanuque G-10 23
Napier H-14 47
Naples (Napoli), Italy D-6 31
Naples, Fl., U.S. M-6 11
Nara E-15 35
Nārāyanganj E-13 39
Narvik B-9 28
Naryn I-13 32
Nāshik E-9 39
Nashville H-3 11
Nassau C-9 17
Nasser, Lake, res. E-13 43
Natal E-11 23
Natchez K-11 13
Natchitoches K-10 13
Natuna Besar, Kepulauan, i. E-4 36
Naturaliste, Cape G-1 46
Nauru, ctry. G-9 44

Navarin, Mys, c. E-33 33
Navoi I-11 32
Navojoa D-5 18
Nayarit, state G-7 18
Nazca F-4 22
N'Djamena G-9 43
Ndola E-5 41
Nebit-Dag J-8 32
Nebraska, state F-6 12
Needles K-7 15
Needles Point H-14 47
Negev Desert o-23 25
Negro, stm., Arg. D-3 21
Negro, stm., Braz. D-6 22
Nei Monggol, prov. C-10 35
Neiva C-3 22
Nellore G-11 39
Nelson I-13 47
Nemunas, stm. D-10 29
Nepal, ctry. D-11 39
Neryungri F-22 33
Netherlands, ctry. F-7 28
Netherlands Antilles, dep. F-11 17
Neuchâtel C-5 30
Neuquén D-3 21
Neuquén, stm. D-3 21
Nevada, state I-6 15
Nevel'sk H-26 33
Nevinnomyssk I-6 32
Nevis, Ben, mtn. D-4 28
New Albany H-2 11
New Amsterdam B-7 23
Newark F-9 10
New Bern I-8 11
New Braunfels L-7 13
New Britain, i. G-13 36
New Brunswick F-9 10
New Brunswick, prov. G-20 7
New Caledonia, dep. E-11 47
New Castle, Pa., U.S. F-6 10
Newcastle, Austl. G-9 47
Newcastle upon Tyne D-5 28
New Delhi D-10 39
Newfoundland, prov. F-21 7
New Glasgow D-8 6
New Guinea, i. F-11 36
New Hampshire, state E-11 10
New Haven F-10 10
New Hebrides, is. D-12 47
New Iberia L-11 13
New Jersey, state F-9 10
New Kowloon (Xinjiulong) s-27 25
New Mexico, state K-11 15
New Orleans L-11 13
New Plymouth H-13 47
Newport, Wales, U.K. E-5 28
Newport, Vt., U.S. D-10 10
Newport Beach L-6 15
New Providence, i. D-9 17
New Siberian Islands B-25 33
New Smyrna Beach L-6 11
New South Wales, state G-7 46
New Ulm D-9 12
New York F-10 10
New York, state E-9 10
New Zealand, ctry. I-13 47
Ngaoundéré H-9 42
Nha Trang C-4 36
Niagara Falls E-7 10
Niamey G-7 42
Nicaragua, ctry. F-8 17
Nicaragua, Lago de, l. F-7 16
Nice D-5 30
Nicobar Islands D-1 36
Nicosia E-10 31
Nieuw Amsterdam B-7 23
Nieuw Nickerie B-7 23
Niger, stm. H-8 42
Niger, ctry. F-9 42
Nigeria, ctry. H-8 42
Nijmegen E-7 28
Nikolayevsk-na-Amure G-26 33
Nikopol' C-10 31
Nile, stm. D-13 43
Niles F-3 10
Nimba, Mount H-5 42
Nîmes D-4 30
Ningbo F-12 35
Ningxia Huizu, prov. D-9 34
Nipigon, Lake G-16 7
Niš D-8 31
Niterói H-10 23
Niue, dep. H-12 45
Nizhevartovsk E-13 32
Nizhneudinsk F-17 33
Nizhniy Novgorod (Gorky) F-6 32
Nizhniy Tagil F-10 32
Nizhnyaya Poyma F-17 33
Nizhnyaya Tunguska, stm. E-14 35
Nkongsamba H-8 42
Nogales, Mex. B-4 18

Nogales, Az., U.S. M-9 15
Noginsk F-5 32
Nome C-3 5
Nordkapp, c. A-11 29
Norfolk, Nb., U.S. F-6 12
Norfolk, Va., U.S. H-8 11
Norfolk Island, dep. E-12 47
Noril'sk D-14 32
Normal F-12 12
Norman I-8 13
Norman Wells F-12 6
North Adams E-10 10
Northampton E-10 10
North America, cont. D-3 2
North Andaman, i. C-1 36
North Bay G-18 7
North Cape G-13 47
North Carolina, state I-7 11
North Channel D-4 28
North Dakota, state C-6 12
Northern Cook Islands G-12 45
Northern Ireland, pol. div. E-4 28
Northern Mariana Islands, ctry. B-12 37
Northern Territory, terr. D-5 46
North Highlands I-4 15
North Island H-13 47
North Korea, ctry. D-13 35
North Las Vegas J-7 15
North Platte F-6 12
North Platte, stm. F-5 12
North Sea D-6 28
North West Cape E-1 46
Northwest Territories D-13 6
Norwalk F-10 10
Norway, ctry. C-7 28
Norway House F-14 6
Norwegian Sea B-6 28
Norwich E-6 28
Nottingham E-5 28
Nouâdhibou E-3 42
Nouadhibou, Ra's, c. E-3 42
Nouakchott E-3 42
Nouméa E-12 47
Nouvelle Calédonie, i. E-12 47
Nova Friburgo H-10 23
Nova Iguaçu H-10 23
Novara C-5 30
Nova Scotia, prov. G-21 7
Novaya Sibir', Ostrov, i. B-27 33
Novaya Zemlya, i. C-9 32
Novgorod F-4 32
Novi Sad C-7 31
Novocherkassk I-5 32
Novo Hamburgo B-6 21
Novokuznetsk G-15 32
Novomoskovsk G-5 32
Novorossiysk I-5 32
Novosibirsk G-14 32
Novyy Port D-12 32
Nueva Rosita D-9 19
Nuevo Laredo D-10 19
Nuevo León, state E-10 19
Nukus I-9 32
Nullarbor Plain G-4 46
Nürnberg C-6 30
Nyasa, Lake E-6 41
Oahe, Lake, res. D-6 12
Oahu, i. i-23 5

O

Oakland J-3 15
Oak Ridge I-4 11
Oamaru J-13 47
Oaxaca I-11 19
Oaxaca, state I-11 19
Ob', stm. E-11 32
Ocala L-5 11
Occidental, Cordillera, mts., Col. C-3 22
Occidental, Cordillera, mts., Peru G-5 22
Ocean City G-9 10
Ocotlán G-5 19
Odense D-8 28
Oder, stm. B-6 31
Odesa C-10 31
Odessa K-5 13
Ofanto, stm. D-7 31
Offenbach C-5 30
Ogaden, region H-15 43
Ogallala F-6 12
Ogbomosho H-7 42
Ogden H-9 15
Ohio, stm. G-5 10
Ohio, state F-5 10
Oise, stm. C-4 30
Ōita E-14 35
Ojos del Salado, Nevado, mtn. B-3 21

Okavango, stm. F-3 41
Okeechobee, Lake M-6 11
Okha G-26 33
Okhotsk, Sea of G-27 33
Okinawa-jima, i. F-13 35
Oklahoma, state I-8 13
Oklahoma City I-8 13
Oktyabr'sk H-9 32
Olavarría D-4 21
Old Crow C-6 6
Oldenburg B-5 30
Oleksandriya C-10 31
Ólimpos, mtn. D-8 31
Olomouc C-7 31
Olsztyn B-8 31
Olympia E-3 14
Olympus, Mount E-3 14
Omaha F-8 12
Oman, ctry. E-6 38
Oman, Gulf of E-6 38
Omdurman (Umm Durmān) F-13 43
Omsk F-12 32
100 Mile House F-9 6
Oneonta E-9 10
Onezhskoye Ozero, l. E-5 32
Onitsha H-8 42
Onslow D-2 46
Ontario, prov. G-16 7
Ontario, Lake E-7 10
Opelousas K-10 13
Opole B-7 31
Opportunity E-8 14
Oradea C-8 31
Orange, stm. H-3 41
Orange Walk H-15 19
Oranjestad F-11 17
Ord, Mount D-4 46
Örebro D-9 28
Oregon, state G-4 14
Orel G-5 32
Orem H-9 15
Orenburg G-9 32
Oriental, Cordillera, mts., Col. C-3 22
Oriental, Cordillera, mts., Peru F-4 22
Orinoco, stm. B-6 23
Orizaba H-11 19
Orizaba, Pico de, vol. H-11 19
Orkney Islands D-5 28
Orlando L-6 11
Orléans C-4 30
Örnsköldsvik C-9 29
Oroville I-4 15
Orsha E-12 29
Orsk G-9 32
Orümīyeh B-3 38
Oruro G-5 22
Ōsaka E-15 35
Osh I-12 32
Oshkosh D-12 12
Oshogbo H-7 42
Osijek C-7 31
Oskaloosa F-10 12
Oslo D-8 28
Osnabrück B-5 30
Osorno E-2 21
Ossa, Mount I-8 47
Östersund C-8 28
Ostrava C-7 31
Oswego E-9 10
Otranto, Strait of, b. D-7 31
Ottawa, Ont., Can. G-18 7
Ottawa, Ks., U.S. G-9 12
Ottumwa F-10 12
Otway, Cape H-7 46
Ouachita Mountains I-9 13
Ouagadougou G-6 42
Ouarâne, region E-4 42
Oubangui (Ubangi), stm. B-3 41
Oujda C-6 42
Oulu B-11 29
Ourinhos A-7 21
Oviedo D-2 30
Owensboro H-3 10
Owen Sound H-17 7
Owen Stanley Range, mts. G-12 37
Owosso E-4 10
Owyhee H-6 14
Oxford D-5 28
Ozark K-4 11
Ozark Plateau H-10 13
Ozarks, Lake of the, res. G-10 12

P

Pacasmayo E-3 22
Pachuca G-10 19
Pacific Ocean C-11 44
Padang F-3 36
Padre Island M-8 13

Paducah H-2 11
Page J-9 15
Pagosa Springs H-3 15
Painted Desert K-9 15
Pakistan, ctry. D-8 39
Palau (Belau), ctry. E-10 37
Palawan, i. D-6 36
Palembang F-3 36
Palermo E-6 31
Palestine K-9 13
Palma E-4 30
Palmas F-9 23
Palmer C-7 5
Palmerston North I-14 47
Palmira C-3 22
Palm Springs L-6 15
Palo Alto J-3 15
Pamir, mts. B-9 38
Pampa, region D-3 21
Pamplona D-3 30
Panamá G-9 17
Panama, ctry. G-8 17
Panamá, Golfo de, b. G-9 17
Panamá, Istmo de, isthmus G-8 17
Panama City K-4 11
Panfilov I-13 32
Pangnirtung C-20 7
Panīpat D-10 39
Papeete H-14 45
Papua, Gulf of G-11 37
Papua New Guinea, ctry. G-12 37
Pará, state E-8 23
Paracel Islands (Xisha Qundao) B-5 36
Paragould H-11 13
Paraguay, stm. A-5 21
Paraguay, ctry. A-5 21
Paraíba, state E-11 23
Paramaribo B-7 23
Paraná C-4 21
Paraná, stm. C-4 21
Paraná, state A-6 21
Paranaíba G-8 23
Paranaguá B-7 21
Paris, France C-4 30
Paris, Il., U.S. G-12 12
Paris, Tn., U.S. H-2 11
Paris, Tx., U.S. J-9 13
Parkersburg G-6 10
Park Rapids C-9 12
Parma, Italy D-6 30
Parma, Oh., U.S. F-6 10
Parnaíba D-10 23
Pärnu D-10 29
Parramatta G-9 47
Paru, stm. D-8 23
Pasadena K-5 15
Pascagoula K-12 13
Passo Fundo B-6 21
Pastaza, stm. D-3 22
Pasto C-3 22
Patagonia, region F-3 21
Paterson F-9 10
Pathein B-1 36
Pathfinder Reservoir G-11 14
Patna D-12 39
Patos E-11 23
Patos, Lagoa dos, b. C-6 21
Patos de Minas G-9 23
Pátrai E-8 31
Pátzcuaro H-9 19
Paulo Afonso E-11 23
Pavlodar G-13 32
Paysandú C-5 21
Peace, stm. E-11 6
Pearl Harbor j-23 5
Peć D-8 31
Pechora D-9 32
Pechora, stm. D-8 32
Pecos K-5 13
Pécs C-7 31
Pedra Azul G-10 23
Pedreiras D-10 23
Pekanbaru E-3 36
Pelly Mountains D-7 6
Pelly Crossing D-6 6
Peloponnesus, i. E-8 31
Pelotas C-6 21
Pemba, i. C-8 41
Pendleton F-5 14
Penedo F-11 23
Pennsylvania, state F-7 11
Penrith G-9 47
Pensacola K-3 11
Pensacola Mountains A-7 48
Penza G-7 32
Penzance E-4 28
Peoria F-12 12
Pereira C-3 22
Pergamino C-4 21
Perm' F-9 32
Pernambuco, state E-11 23